THE BOOK
OF
BUFFALO
POTTERY

Rectangular platter 14 by 11 inches shows "Dr. Syntax Advertisement for a Wife." *Courtesy of the Buffalo and Erie County Historical Society.*

THE BOOK
OF
BUFFALO
POTTERY

by

Violet and Seymour Altman

BONANZA BOOKS · NEW YORK

PHOTOGRAPHY BY STANLEY S. FURRY
Designed by Shari de Miskey

© MCMLXIX, by Violet and Seymour Altman
Library of Congress Catalog Card Number: 70–75071

This edition published by Bonanza Books
a division of Crown Publishers, Inc.,
a b c d e f g h

*We dedicate this book to our three
children—Renee, Alan, and Joyce—
without whose patience, cooperation,
and understanding over the past
three years, this book would not
have been possible*

Manufactured in the United States of America

Contents

Foreword

Countless hours and untold effort have gone into the gathering of information concerning two Buffalo companies that have contributed much to the mores of marketing in America.

John D. Larkin and Elbert Hubbard were familiar names to an earlier generation of Americans, as they established methods of selling that are common practice today.

Both the Larkin Company and Buffalo Pottery, now Buffalo China, Inc., have been important contributors to the economy of Buffalo, as well as major factors in their industries.

We, who have been identified through the years with these companies, are particularly pleased that the authors have shared our belief that the story of these companies is so interesting one could write a book about it. Because of the increasing tempo of change in the chinaware industry, in which Buffalo China is a pacesetter, it was necessary for an outsider, someone who loved history and cherished collectors' items, someone who could look backward to gather together the strands of this story, to undertake this work.

We have been amazed at the diligence of the authors and their ability to ferret out many unusual and little-known items of interest. We know of their search of historical archives and newspaper records and their many interviews with persons familiar with an era long past. This thoroughness should be a testimony to the accuracy of their authorship where we, the descendants of the founder, cannot document and corroborate every little fact in the manuscript. In a work of this nature, however, we can imagine little or no incentive for anyone to distort or embellish the facts.

This book, we hope, will serve as a sound foundation for the ongoing history of Buffalo China. We shall make every effort to keep better records of our activities in the future so that when this story is updated at some later time, perhaps during Buffalo's seventy-fifth anniversary in 1976, the authors will not have to search so hard.

We hope, too, that this book will give the readers an insight into the manufacture of chinaware in the United States, and enrich their lives with a fuller appreciation of this industry.

HAROLD M. ESTY, JR.
HARRY H. LARKIN, JR.

Buffalo, New York
March, 1969

Acknowledgments

Most of the photographs in this book are the work of our friend and associate Stanley S. Furry. Almost all Buffalo pottery has an extremely brilliant glaze, which reflects light like a mirror—a serious and exasperating problem for Stan, but his complete dedication to our project won out in the end. A very special thanks goes to him for his willingness to cooperate far beyond the call of duty, and to Beverly Furry, his wife, for the many evenings he spent away from home to work on our photographs.

We are deeply grateful also to Harold M. Esty, Jr., president of Buffalo China, and Harry H. Larkin, Jr., grandson of the founder of the Larkin Company, for their interest, kindness, and aid.

Among the scores of others who helped us in one way or another, the following deserve special mention and our sincere thanks:

Mr. Clare Allen
Mr. and Mrs. Franz Bach
The Baltimore & Ohio Railroad
The British Museum
Lawrence Brown
Buffalo Courier Express
Buffalo Evening News
Buffalo Historical Society
Buffalo Public Library
Louise Carney
Mrs. Emanuel Cascio
The Chesapeake and Ohio Railroad
Mrs. Ada Jane Corbett
Mrs. Thomas Cornell
Mr. and Mrs. Robert L. Crane
Mr. and Mrs. Pat Cutini
Oscar Dale
Churchill DeWitt
Thomas Doncaster
Mrs. Gertrude Doyle
East Aurora Historical
    Society
Mrs. Mabel Gerhardt (Deldare
    decorator)
Mrs. Alice R. Herrmann
Bertha Hyden
Rix Jennings
Anna Kappler (original employee)
Mrs. Emil Klein
Fred Krausen (engraver and
    decorator)
Mrs. Winnie Kurtz
Marguerite Marquardt
Tobio Martino
Agnes Masters

David Meek
Joseph Meidel
The Metropolitan Museum of Art
Mrs. John Meyers
Francis Murray
Mr. and Mrs. John Navaugh
Arthur Nenstiel
Mr. and Mrs. Lawrence M. Nicholson
Dr. and Mrs. John Prout
Mrs. Clara Rappold
Mrs. August Riehs
Mrs. Walter B. Robb
Barry Rodgers
Mr. and Mrs. Edward Rowan
Sagamore Hill National Historic Site
June Salvatore
Mr. and Mrs. Charles Sprenger
State University of New York at
    Buffalo
Beth Stegner
Chris Stegner
Adele Steinagle
Mr. and Mrs. Ralph Stuart
Mrs. Ralph Stuart, Sr.
Mrs. Franklin W. Tripp
Jane Van Arsdale
Anna Vogel
Bertha Vogel
Esther Vogel
Flora Vogel
Maude Waver
Cora Webster
Charles White
Frank L. Withee
Carolyn Wood

Introduction

Why a book on Buffalo pottery? If you had ever sought information of any kind about this subject, you would know the reason. Various brief articles about the pottery and its wares have appeared in magazines, it is true, but most of these have presented only a minimum of information, and have been laced with inaccuracies. Therefore, in spite of the frustrations and difficulties we encountered in researching the subject, we felt that such a book was both imperative and long overdue.

As far as we know, this is the first attempt to compile a full-length book on Buffalo pottery. Being native Buffalonians, still living in the city where the pottery originated, we believed we were in a unique position to do extensive research into the history of the company and its products. Nonetheless, in spite of our advantageous location, we were amazed to discover how little is known about this company whose history is comparatively recent and whose wares are not as yet true antiques, though they are widely sought-after collectors' items. Today, the products of this pottery, especially the Deldare Ware, are being collected with increasing eagerness, at constantly rising prices. In fact, few other collectors' items, antique or not, enjoy the popularity of Buffalo pottery; and it is our belief that this popularity will increase in the future and the prices continue to soar, for these wares are well on the road to becoming tomorrow's antiques.

The process of gathering information and specimens of Buffalo pottery for this book was (as we have implied) marked by many problems. For one thing, such a book should have been written, or the materials gathered, many years ago before most of the people who could have told the complete story of the pottery had died. The few who now remain are well along in years—too old to remember all the details with any great degree of accuracy. The last ten years in particular have taken a heavy toll among the original key employees.

The lack of documented materials was also a severe stumbling block. The pottery seems to have kept few records of the items produced there, of the method of manufacture, the processes of decoration, the volume of each type of ware produced, the dates when each series was originated and discontinued, and the reasons why. Records of this kind were kept originally, but in the various modernization and expansion programs over the years, these records were destroyed. Practically none are available today from Buffalo China, the successors to Buffalo Pottery, or from surviving employees. Sales catalogs and brochures are also practically nonexistent, and those that do exist cover only a small proportion of the products manufactured in earlier years. Apparently, nostalgia went out of fashion when mass production became the watchword. (For the last twenty-five years, almost the entire pottery output has been mass-produced wares that cannot be considered collectible.) The best indication of what was made at the pottery in the old days is probably to be found in the premium catalogs published by the Larkin Company—but even these do not show everything.

A large part of the information given in this book was accumulated by exhausting legwork. In the more than three years spent on research, we traveled countless miles and interviewed over two hundred people, not only employees of the company but also surviving relatives of employees and anyone who had been even remotely connected with the pottery. Some of our scheduled interviews failed to materialize—for sad reasons. For example, we were planning a trip to Florida in May, 1967, to talk to the widow of Ralph Stuart, head artist at the pottery for many years, when we received word that Mrs. Stuart had passed away suddenly and unexpectedly at the age of eighty-four. She herself had also been an employee of the pottery at one time—one of the best Deldare decorators. Her maiden name, Anna Delaney, can be found on many pieces of Deldare. She had met her husband while they were both working at the pottery. Fortunately, we had previously talked to Mrs. Stuart by phone, and she had given us some information, but we are sure that with her death many facts about the pottery are now lost forever.

As a general rule, most of the people we talked to were cooperative, freely giving us whatever information they possessed. A few, however, were adamant in refusing us aid. Their attitude was understandable. The incidence of silicosis among the employees, caused by the high content of clay dust in the air at the plant, resulted in many deaths. The survivors of some of these employees thus have unhappy memories of the pottery, and were hesitant to discuss it. We did not press them. Other employees refused to give information for various reasons. Hence, we are the more deeply indebted to those who were cooperative and provided us with enough information so that we could complete this book.

Besides bringing to the public a sorely needed reference source, it has been our aim in preparing this book to acquaint collectors, dealers, and historians with both the variety and beauty of the wares manufactured at the Buffalo Pottery. Many people do not know that the factory produced other items besides the Deldare for which it is so famous. While we were collecting specimens (mostly Deldare), we were repeatedly amazed at the diversification of the wares that turned up. Almost every time we set out on a search, we came up with something we did not know existed.

Another of our aims was to perpetuate the memory of the Larkin Company and of the Buffalo Pottery in the permanent annals of the city of Buffalo. These two industrial institutions are a part of the city's heritage. The motto of the Buffalo Chamber of Commerce is "Boost Buffalo," and we hope our book will serve to that end.

In spite of all the hard work that went into the compilation of the book, we can say in all honesty that the task was not without its happy moments and its satisfactions. Though we do not profess any literary talents, we have tried to the best of our abilities to make the book informative, interesting, complete, and historically accurate. We earnestly hope the reader will find it has all those qualities.

Vi and Si Altman

1. John D. Larkin, 1845–1926. *Courtesy of Harry H. Larkin, Jr.*

2. A page from the Larkin catalog of 1906 pictures the various factories that produced premiums, as well as the evolution of the Larkin Company buildings. The original Larkin factory is in the center. *Courtesy of Harry H. Larkin, Jr.*

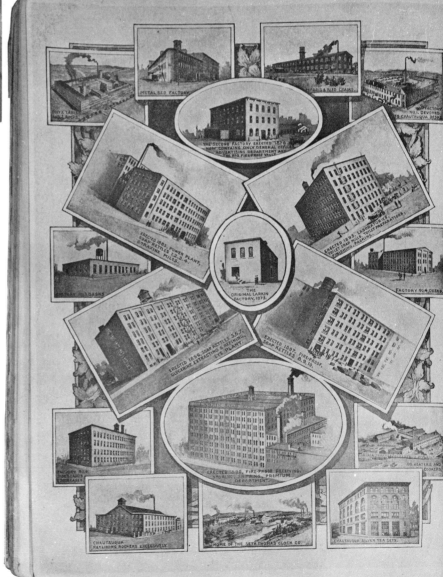

1

The Larkin Company

A BAR OF COMMON LAUNDRY SOAP USUALLY CONTAINS A NUMBER OF RELATIVELY ordinary ingredients, but Larkin Company's Sweet Home Soap had greater significance than most such simple combinations of chemicals: it was the product responsible for the birth of one of the foremost potteries in the United States.

John Durrant Larkin (Ill. 1), the son of English immigrants, was born in Buffalo, New York, on September 29, 1845. His parents, Levi Henry Larkin and Mary Durrant, had come to this country in 1832. When John was seven years old, he and his six brothers and sisters were left fatherless. John continued to go to school (Public School 10) until he was twelve, but then it became necessary for him to help support the family. His first job was as a messenger boy for Western Union Telegraph Company; later, he clerked in a wholesale millinery store.

It was not until John Larkin was sixteen (1861) that he was initiated into the manufacturing of soap. At that time he went to work for a man named Justus Weller, who operated a local factory. In 1870, Weller sold his Buffalo plant and moved to Chicago with the intention of establishing a soap factory there. John went along. By 1871, he had become a partner in the new enterprise, and he continued his association with Weller until 1875.

In 1874, while he was still in Illinois, John met and married Hannah Frances Hubbard. She too had been born in Buffalo, when her father, Dr. Silas Hubbard, was a practicing physician there. But the Hubbards had later moved to Bloomington, Illinois, and it was there that their second child, a son named Elbert, had been born in 1856.

Young Larkin was anxious to establish a soap business of his own, and so in 1875 he sold his interest in the Weller firm and returned to Buffalo. Almost immediately, he began the manufacture of soap in a small two-story building at 199 Chicago Street (Ill. 2). The business was known as John D. Larkin Company. Its only product, called Sweet Home Soap, was a variety of yellow laundry soap. This was marketed by peddlers who used handcarts to trundle their wares along the streets of Buffalo. Larkin's soap was of good quality, and it was cheaper than competitors' soaps, so it found a ready market both among merchants and with the general public. To facilitate sales, the Larkin Company would, at a merchant's request, imprint the wrappers and the bars of soap with his name, giving the public the impression that the soap was the merchant's own special brand. Generous samples were distributed to acquaint potential customers with the Larkin product.

From the beginning, John Larkin was fortunate in having as associates men of considerable business ability. William H. and Daniel J. Coss joined him in 1875. They handled production in the new factory, and did a very thorough job of it until 1909. He was also fortunate in having Elbert Hubbard, his brother-in-law, as his first salesman. Hubbard's genius for descriptive writing and sales promotion was evident in the advertising propaganda of the Larkin Company. It was probably his talent for merchandismg, more than any other single factor, that was responsible for the growth of the company, which was unusually rapid. By 1876, Larkin already had to seek larger quarters, and he had a new three-story plant, 50 by 150 feet, built at 663 Seneca Street. Two years later, Hubbard became a partner in the firm, and the name was changed to J. D. Larkin and Company. At this time (1878), Darwin D. Martin entered the firm.

Not only had the capacity of the plant been expanded; new products were soon added. In 1879, a washing fluid called Sweet Home followed the soap of that name. Boraxine, a soap powder, joined the list in 1881. With the marketing of Boraxine, an innovation was introduced that started the company on the way to fame: In each box of the soap powder a chromo picture was inserted as a bonus or premium. Giving premiums was not a new practice—providing coupons that could be accumulated and exchanged for premiums was a widespread merchandising custom. It was the inclusion of the premium directly in or with a purchase that was the Larkin Company innovation. Henceforth, all new products introduced by the company included a premium as a buying incentive.

In 1883 toilet soaps were added to the Larkin line. The best known of these was Pure White, which retailed at twenty-five cents (for a twelve-cake box) and had a handkerchief enclosed in each box. Pure White was soon being referred to by the public as "handkerchief soap." In 1883, Ocean Bath Soap included a bath towel as a premium. Another popular item was Creme Oatmeal Soap, which was first sold to the trade by traveling salesmen, but shortly after was sold by printed circulars mailed directly to merchants. In the Elegant Eighties, French names and spellings were the vogue, and that was what inspired Hubbard to choose the name "Creme Oatmeal."

It was L. F. Martin, oldest brother of Darwin Martin, who gave Hubbard the idea of packaging a three-cake box of toilet soap to retail at ten cents a box. Like many good ideas, this one was born of necessity. It was sometimes difficult to get merchants to buy toilet soaps put up twelve cakes to a box. The dime was a popular coin then, and when the idea of marketing a three-cake box of soap for that price was proposed at a sales meeting, Hubbard at once saw its merits. He submitted the plan to Larkin, and samples of a three-cake pack were quickly made. The paper boxes were lined with lace paper, but the thin, unseasoned cakes of soap were not wrapped. Merchants readily recognized the salability of the new package, and large orders began pouring in from all parts of the country. In fact, it was not long before Hubbard realized that sales could easily be made by mail solicitation, without the aid of traveling salesmen. L. F. Martin's bright idea proved so successful that, in time, he and the rest of the salesmen were eliminated by the Larkin Company. This first Larkin mail-order business, it should be pointed out, was with merchants rather than directly with the consumer.

The popularity of Creme Oatmeal Soap taxed the capacity of the little three-story factory at 663 Seneca Street. To keep up with the orders, both a day and night shift of workers was required—until an expansion was completed in 1885, a new building 64 by 100 feet, five stories high, that cost $12,000. This structure replaced the rear frame building and extended over a newly acquired adjoining lot. Pleased with their enlarged quarters and freedom from night-shift work, little did the employees of that day realize that greater expansions would eventually be necessary and that within twenty-five years the company would annually be selling 175 million bars of yellow laundry soap and 1½ million bars of toilet soap.

In 1885, Boraxine was again used for a marketing experiment: the wrappers were to be saved and eventually redeemed for premiums. To attract more customers and make the accumulation of wrappers more appealing, the company realized that they had to increase the number and variety of premiums offered. It was at about this period that direct selling became of prime interest to the organization—the "Factory to Family" method of marketing.

The Larkin idea was to sell directly to the consumer—with no dealers at all, wholesale or retail, and no traveling salesmen or brokers. They aimed to eliminate the middleman completely, and sell important staples on a large scale entirely to the consumer. Such a procedure would save "all cost that adds no value." The profits that would have been realized by the middleman under the old method of sales were henceforth to be transferred to the buyer in the form of premiums. A customer who bought ten dollars' worth of soap at retail price would be entitled to a premium of that value as well. Thus, for ten dollars, he would be receiving a twenty-dollar value.

Reaction to this theory of merchandising was immediate. Businessmen considered it rash, and merchants refused to handle Larkin goods. The old heads in the soap business laughed at the plan because they were so certain it would not work. Besides, they saw no good reason for giving the consumer merchandise he was not paying for. But the Larkin Company idea persisted—and it grew and grew.

In the summer of 1886, Hubbard's fertile mind conceived an entirely new method of merchandising. This was known as a "Combination Box," which sold for six dollars. It contained one hundred cakes of Sweet Home Soap, and, as premiums, an assortment of other soaps and various products that would be useful to the average consumer, who would be allowed thirty days in which to pay the six dollars. The plan created such a problem in handling sales accounts that they could not be kept in the usual bound ledgers, and a system using index cards was introduced—a card ledger. The Larking Company is credited with being the first in the world to make such a ledger. Instead of destroying a card after the account was paid, Hubbard decided to save all the cards; they became the nucleus of a gigantic mailing list.

Following is a list of the premiums included in each Combination Box:

> 6 silver-plated teaspoons
> 1 child's silver-plated teaspoon
> 1 silver-plated napkin ring
> 2 silver-plated single butter plates
> 1 silver-plated butter plate
> 3 bars Artistic Toilet Soap
> 3 bars Elite Toilet Soap
> 3 bars Creme Oatmeal Toilet Soap
> 3 bars Ideal Toilet Soap
> 3 bars Ocean Bath Soap
> 3 bars Modjeska Toilet Soap

In 1889, the Larkin Company sold 94,000 Combination Boxes. Later, it was found to be more economical to ship a ten-dollar Combination Box instead of the six-dollar box, and so this amount became standard. Each ten-dollar box contained the following:

> 100 cakes of Sweet Home Soap
> 11 boxes Boraxine
> 1 Modjeska Complexion Soap
> 1 bottle Modjeska Perfume
> 1 box Ocean Bath Toilet Soap
> 1 box Creme Oatmeal Soap
> 1 box Elite Toilet Soap
> 1 English jar of Modjeska Cold Cream

14

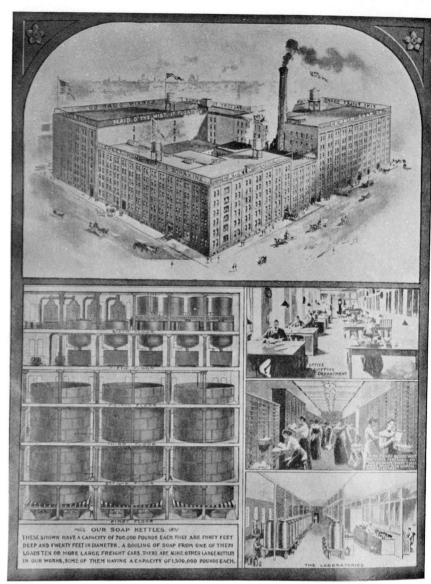

3. The Larkin catalog of 1903 devoted a full page to showing customers the immense factory and the gigantic five-story soap vats. *Courtesy of Harry H. Larkin, Jr.*

> 1   bottle Modjeska Tooth Powder
> 1   packet satchet powder
> 1   stick shaving soap

The premium given with this Combination Box was either a Chautauqua desk or Chautauqua lamp, which also had a value of ten dollars. If cash was paid in advance, some gift for the lady of the house would be included with the above. All boxes were sent on a thirty-day trial basis, with the freight being prepaid. If the customer was not satisfied with the contents, he could return the unopened packages, and he need not pay for the packages he had used. Boxes ordered around Christmas always contained extra presents, and were eagerly awaited by the customer. Sometimes money was preferred to a premium, and in such cases one dollar was given for each order, providing that five or more orders were sent simultaneously.

Combination Boxes, as such, disappeared in the first decade of the twentieth century. The Larkin order still had to amount to ten dollars, but the customer was allowed to select any desired assortment of the products offered, as well as the premium he preferred.

Another method devised for selling was the "Larkin Club." Ten housewives could form a club, each one contributing a dollar monthly. This purchased one Combination Box, and the women drew lots for the premium. In reality, the club was a means of purchasing on the installment plan, although at this period

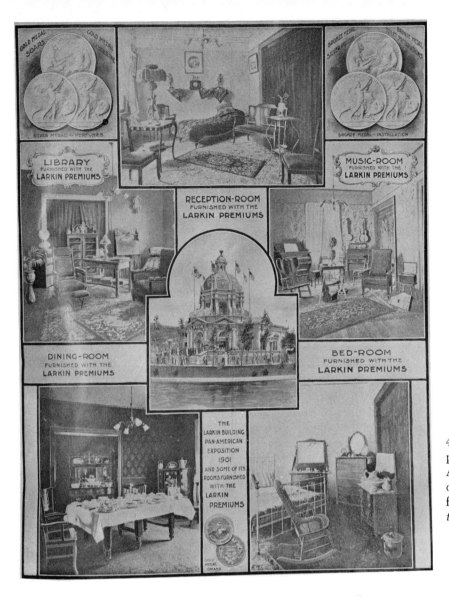

4. Another page of the 1903 catalog pictured the Larkin Pavilion at the Pan-American Exposition of 1901, and some of the rooms in that building that were furnished with Larkin premiums. *Courtesy of Harry H. Larkin, Jr.*

installment buying was frowned upon. However, the club plan was the heart of the distribution of the Larkin mail-order business and one of the biggest factors in the success of the company.

The first large premium was the Chautauqua piano lamp, a tall brass kerosene lamp with a silk shade. Next came a Chautaqua desk, then a Chautaqua chair; following them, a Chautauqua stove. To inform customers of an enlarged choice of premiums, the Larkin Company published their first catalogue on July 1, 1893. Prior to this, individual flyers had been issued for each item, but thereafter the company published catalogs frequently. The premium catalog of 1905 listed almost 900 varied items from which a customer could choose. From 1909 on, two catalogs were sent each year (fall/winter, and spring/summer)—a million and a half each time. To mail these three million messengers of home improvement every year, along with the five million folders and letters broadcasting the Larkin idea, and the vast parcel-post package mail, Uncle Sam maintained a branch post office right in the Larkin plant. The daily order mail of Larkin Company and its branches also poured in by the thousands to this post office, giving evidence of the pleasure and satisfaction of dealing with Larkin. Little wonder that the Larkin catalog was called "The Book of a Million Homes."

In February, 1892, the Larkin Soap Manufacturing Company was formed with a capitalization of $500,000, an enormous sum for this period. John Larkin was elected president, and Elbert Hubbard, secretary and treasurer. About a year later, just past thirty-five years of age, Hubbard decided to retire from the Larkin Company and devote himself to more artistic pursuits. After trying college, a job with a publishing company, and a European tour during which he came to be a great admirer of William Morris, he returned to western New York and in 1895 set up a colony of artisans called The Roycrofters, in the town of East Aurora, not far from Buffalo. The colony, patterned on the philosophy of Morris, aimed at reviving old handicrafts, particularly those associated with printing, bookbinding, leather craft, metalworking and woodworking.

Hubbard also became known as a writer, best remembered today perhaps for his *A Message to Garcia*, written in 1899, which sold forty million copies. In his own time, he achieved wide attention also as the publisher and editor (and largely the writer) of two small magazines, the *Philistine* and the *Fra*, and of *Little Journeys*, monthly pamphlets that eventually filled fourteen volumes.

Hubbard and his wife were lost when the *Lusitania* was torpedoed by a German submarine in 1915.

Hubbard's resignation seemed to have little effect on the continued rapid growth of the Larkin Company. Almost yearly, after 1877, there was further expansion—old buildings gave way to new ones, small ones to large ones; common brick and wood were replaced with fireproof construction—until the available floor space in the Larkin plant was of incredible extent. Little more than an acre in 1885, it had increased to over sixteen acres by 1901, over twenty-nine by 1904, fifty by 1907, and more than sixty-four acres by 1914. Enormous shipments left daily from the Larkin Terminal Buildings, destined for all points of the compass. As the company grew, branches and warehousing facilities (Ill. 7) were built in Peoria, New York, Philadelphia, Pittsburgh, Cleveland, Chicago, and Los Angeles, but the branch offices were short-lived. Improvements in transportation and parcel-post services made them unnecessary.

The Buffalo Chamber of Commerce once stated in a publication that the local plant of the Larkin Company was the world's largest manufactory of soaps (Ill. 3), perfumes, toilet preparations, and pure food specialties. Whether this statement was accurate, or somewhat biased in the interest of publicizing Buffalo, is difficult to decide, but the immensity of the Larkin plant and operations seems to indicate that they must have been among the largest of their kind at that time. The employees numbered more than twenty-five hundred, and the company's purchases of raw and manufactured materials must have been responsible for the employment of thousands more.

In 1903, John D. Larkin recognized the desirability of consolidating all secretarial and administrative operations of the company under one roof. Frank Lloyd Wright (the controversial architect was at the time building homes for a number of Larkin executives in Buffalo) was commissioned to draft plans for a new building (Ill. 5). Since this was the first commercial structure Wright had done, the commission represented both a challenge and an opportunity for him; nonetheless, he insisted on having full power to execute the interior of the building also—the furniture, lighting equipment, decorations, and so on (Ill. 6).

The new Larkin Administration Building achieved wide fame not only in the United States but also in Europe, where it was often pictured in books on architecture. It was one of the largest private office buildings in the world at that time, and one of the best planned for efficiency as well. Its size can be gauged from the fact that it provided working space for 1,800 clerks and typists and all the company executives and their secretaries. Lighting and ventilation equipment, restaurant facilities and rest rooms—all were of the most modern design. To give the staff still greater pleasure in their working conditions, John D. Larkin celebrated the firm's fiftieth anniversary in 1925 by installing a gigantic $90,000 pipe

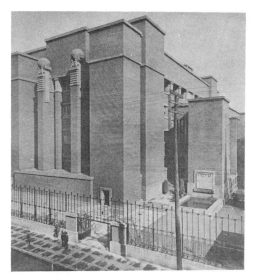

5. Larkin Company Administration Building designed by Frank Lloyd Wright in 1904. *Courtesy of Harry H. Larkin, Jr.*

6. Interior view of Larkin Administration Building showing some of the furnishings designed by Frank Lloyd Wright. *Courtesy of Harry H. Larkin, Jr.*

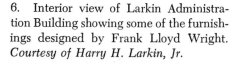

7. Larkin factories and branches as shown in the catalog of 1914. *Courtesy of Harry H. Larkin, Jr.*

8. A cuspidor used in the Larkin buildings. It was made by Buffalo Pottery. *Courtesy of Harry H. Larkin, Jr.*

organ that would provide them with background music to work by. This was one of the dozen largest organs in the United States at the time.

In 1967, during an interview with Harry H. Larkin, Jr., at the Larkin Warehouse (the last remaining building of the Larkin complex then still owned by the family), the authors had the privilege of examining some of the original office chairs designed by Frank Lloyd Wright. We were surprised at their stiff and uncomfortable look, and downright amazed at the fortitude of any secretary who could sit on such a chair for an entire workday. The Larkin Administration Building fell under the wrecking ball in 1950. The warehouse that we visited, along with the furniture that had been stored. there, was disposed of shortly after our visit.

In the early years after the turn of the century, the general public was invited to visit the Larkin complex and see the various operations. The response was gratifying, for titled foreigners—the King and Queen of Belgium, for instance— were as interested in inspecting the Larkin setup as the average American. By far the majority of the visitors, however, were people who had dealt with the Larkin Company for years and profited by the Larkin idea. In 1908 alone, upward of 50,000 people from all over the world took the conducted tour through the Larkin buildings. Everyone was made to feel welcome and at home, shown everything they wanted to see and much that they had had no idea of seeing, and also things that they were not likely to see in any other place. From "Inspiration Point" in the Administration Building they had a glimpse of the nerve center of the whole mammoth establishment. At the end of the tour, each visitor was given a souvenir and a cordial invitation to return.

To the company's original soap product and its by-product, glycerin, Larkin gradually added perfumes and pharmaceuticals until, by 1900, they were manufacturing all these products. In time, the company became involved in other quite diversified manufacturing enterprises. There was a good reason for this. First of all, as mentioned earlier, the premium plan required a variety of products in quite large quantities, and Larkin found it both convenient and profitable to produce these articles for themselves. Second, since most mail-order customers desired other goods besides soap and soap products, Larkin expanded in the directions where the demand was the greatest—that is, into the manufacture of various types of packaged foods such as coffee, tea, and extracts. By 1906, the company had also begun to manufacture paints and varnishes, and then went into the making of furniture. Added next to the list were textiles, including such garments as house dresses, aprons, and children's clothes. Then came a bakery, to supply all the bread, cake, and pastry sold in the company's retail stores.

In addition to all the manufacturing carried on in the Larkin plants, it was still necessary to have outside factories produce certain items. A leather company supplied Larkin with leather goods and shoes. A furniture company in Memphis, Tennessee, near a source of lumber, produced furniture parts and sent them to Buffalo for finishing. Bottles and other glass articles were made for Larkin by the Greenburg Glass Company in Greenburg, Pennsylvania. Larkin was also associated with the Buffalo Garment Company, manufacturer of men's apparel.

Last but not least, in 1901 the Larkin Company founded the Buffalo Pottery Company to produce dishes and other ceramic articles, both for premium use and general sale. So it came about—as stated at the beginning of this chapter— that an art pottery developed as a result of a successful cake of laundry soap.

Today the Goliath that was once the Larkin Company no longer exists. All that remains of the vast enterprise is the weathered inscription "Larkin Company" chiseled into the once-proud structures.

2

The Buffalo Pottery

THE LARKIN COMPANY, AS ALREADY MENTIONED, REQUIRED A CONSIDERABLE AMOUNT of pottery and china to satisfy its premium needs. Merchandise of the quality Larkin desired was expensive, and depending on an outside firm for prompt delivery had its hazards. More than once, the idea crossed Larkin's mind: why not establish a pottery of his own?

Among the china salesmen who called regularly at Larkin Company was one Louis Bown, representing the Crescent Pottery of Trenton, New Jersey. Bown and Larkin had many conversations about the feasibility of setting up a pottery in Buffalo, and at length Larkin took the first step—applying for a charter. The charter was issued on October 23, 1901. At the first stockholders' meeting, held on October 28 of that year, John D. Larkin was elected president, a position he held until his death in 1926, when his son John D. Larkin, Jr., succeeded him. Charles Larkin was elected vice-president, D. D. Martin, secretary, and John Larkin, Jr., treasurer. It was resolved "To authorize the President to contract for and purchase, or lease, such lands as necessary to erect and equip such a plant as in his judgment, the need of the company demands."

The Buffalo Pottery was capitalized at fifty thousand dollars. A site was purchased at the southeast corner of Seneca and Fillmore streets, but after due consideration was abandoned as inadequate; later the Buffalo Leather Company plant was erected there by Larkin. The search for land continued, and finally a suitable site was bought—a tract eight and a half acres in extent at Seneca Street and Hayes Place. The location was ideal, the land bordering the tracks of the Pennsylvania, Lehigh, and Lackawanna railroads. Robert J. Reidpath, a local structural engineer, was given a contract to lay out and design the buildings. Ground was broken in the spring of 1902, and construction completed in 1903. The firing of the first kiln took place in October, 1903.

Louis Bown quit his sales position with the New Jersey pottery to become Buffalo Pottery's first general manager. Wanting experienced potters to get the new facility off to a proper beginning, Bown brought with him from New Jersey William J. Rea, who was made the first superintendent of production, and a number of other craftsmen. Rea had started his ceramic career at the age of fourteen at the Mayer China Company in Beaver Falls, Pennsylvania. He had also managed a pottery in Tiffin, Ohio, before he became manager of the Trenton

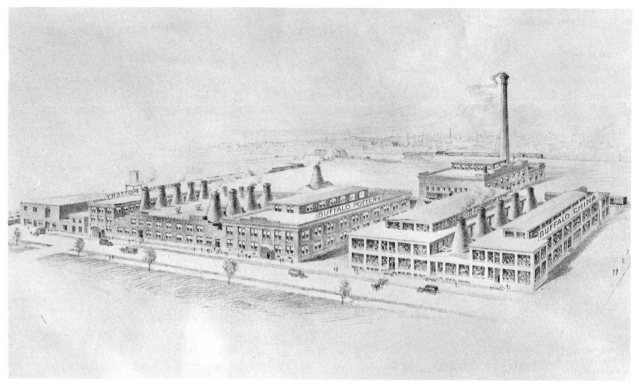

9. General offices and factories of the Buffalo Pottery in 1917. The kilns on the right marked "Buffalo China" were just completed that year.

10. An early photograph of some of the employees in Buffalo Pottery's printshop. *Courtesy of Thomas Doncaster.*

firm for ten years. This skilled man had a good deal of practical knowledge of ceramics, and he had long dreamed of designing and heading a pottery. Buffalo Pottery was built under his direction and to his specifications.

Rea not only produced good pottery but endeavored constantly to raise its quality, especially that of underglaze ware. It was through his endeavors that the firm manufactured America's first Blue Willow. Rea retired on August 27, 1927, after twenty-four years' continuous service at Buffalo Pottery. Both he and Bown eventually became directors of the company, and Bown became vice-president. Rea died in 1942, at the age of seventy-eight.

Other knowledgeable and experienced employees were recruited from various potteries throughout the country. Most such skilled help was paid on a piece-work basis, and a conscientious worker could make an excellent wage. Hence, it was not long before potters from many places were seeking employment at Buffalo Pottery. Soon there was a staff of about two hundred and fifty.

Of the employees who came from New Jersey with Bown at the start, there is only one surviving at the time this is written. She is Mrs. Anna Kappler, who still resides three blocks from the pottery. At eighty-seven, alert and well, she fondly recalls the fifty-three pleasant years she spent with the firm, where she was "foreman" of the printshop.

Among the job seekers who early came to the new pottery was Ralph Stuart, a ceramic artist of the highest caliber. He had been an employee of the Onondaga Pottery Works in Syracuse, but a report of the high piecework rates paid by the Buffalo firm seemed worth investigating. Hired in 1903, he brought with him a rich heritage of ceramic experience: he, his father, and his grandfather before him had worked at some of the leading potteries in the Staffordshire District of England. Stuart himself is said to have worked at Wedgwood and also at the Royal Doulton works. He was related to Gilbert Stuart, who painted the renowned portrait of George Washington. It was this portrait that was used on the George Washington plate (Ill. 275).

Stuart advanced rapidly at Buffalo, eventually becoming head of the Art Department, overseeing printshop, lining, decals, and hand painting. In addition to his duties at the pottery, he taught art and held painting classes at his home, which were attended by many local residents. He was an avid fisherman, hunter, and outdoorsman in his spare time, and it may have been this interest in wildlife that led him to make the paintings of birds, animals, fish, and flowers that were reproduced on many of the Buffalo wares.

Murals of Stuart's still remain today on the dining-room walls of the Arcade Hotel, in Arcade, New York. Over the years, he gave hand-painted Buffalo Pottery pieces of his own design to friends and fellow employees for such occasions as weddings, showers, and similar happy events. While interviewing former employees of the pottery, the authors had the opportunity of examining a number of these special pieces, and without exception found them outstanding in beautiful detail and color—leaving the impression that, had Stuart chosen to devote all his energies to a career as a serious artist, his work might be hanging in museums today. However, except for a tour of duty with the Canadian Army during World War I, he carried on as chief of Buffalo Pottery decorators until 1942, when he left to enter private business. Stuart died in 1945, at the age of sixty-eight.

The eight original buildings on Hayes Place formed the largest fireproof pottery in the world at that time. Substantially constructed of brick, steel, and concrete, they provided some eighty thousand square feet of floor space. Over four hundred windows and skylights let in an abundance of light and fresh air. Buffalo was then the only pottery in the world operated entirely by electricity; an adjoining powerhouse supplied the power to light and heat all the buildings.

Raw materials used by the pottery came not only from all over America but from the Old World as well. Careful attention was given to every detail of handling these materials that might contribute to economy of production and make it possible to turn out quality ware at minimum cost. For example, clays from such widespread sources as North Carolina, Georgia, Florida, Tennessee, Kentucky, Pennsylvania, New Jersey, and Great Britain, and likewise silica, feldspar, borax, kaolin, whiting, leads, oxide of cobalt, and numerous other ingredients, were handled only when they were loaded at the point of shipment or the port of arrival in this country. At the Buffalo plant they were unloaded directly into bins provided for them, in keeping with the idea that from the time a material started on the journey from its source, until it became part of a dainty bit of tableware ready for use in the home, there was not to be a wasted motion.

From the receiving bins, clay and other ingredients moved to the scales on which the proper proportions were weighed out. Then the mass was conveyed by carrier to large vats, where water was added. An energetic plunger played havoc with the lumps, converting the stiff clay into what is known as "slip." In consistency and color, as it streamed from the mixing vats, this looked a good deal like cream. Next the slip passed to the "lawn," as the potters called it; laymen would be more likely to refer to it as a sieve, for its duties were like those of a sieve. The lawn was silk bolting cloth with 15,000 meshes to the square inch, stretched on a frame. Every bit of clay used in the pottery first passed, in the form of slip, through these fine silken meshes.

From the lawn, the clay flowed into a reservoir in which a constantly revolving agitator kept the ingredients of the liquid mass in suspension, until it could be pumped into the filter, or "clay press." Between the iron leaves of the clay press were double thicknesses of army duck cloth. When the slip reached this fabric, the water filtered through the cloth, and dropped, clean and colorless, into pans, which emptied into a well whence the water was pumped up to be used again in the mixing vats. The clay was left impressed between the sheets of duck cloth —in moist square cakes about an inch and a half thick. When the press was opened, these dropped to a truck and were wheeled to the next stopping place, the clay cellar. Here, the clay mellowed. To be left in the cellar a year would help it a great deal; to remain there a hundred years would have helped it still more. After a reasonably thorough mellowing, the clay went into the pug mill in "junks" cut out by a shovel from the supply in the cellar. In the mill it was so cut and pressed and kneaded that when it emerged at the bottom, it was somewhat suggestive of a huge sausage in appearance. Actually, it had become a soft, unctuous paste ready for the potters' deft manipulations, ready to be given a form.

A portion of clay, enough to make a vessel or object, could readily be detached and placed over or in a mold, according to the shape of the piece desired. This use of a mold to give shape to the clay was in direct contrast to the old method of throwing and turning a piece on the wheel, in which it was the fingers and hands of the potter that gave a vessel its rough shape as it was whirled about. After such a rough shape had hardened sufficiently, it would be placed on the wheel again, and the potter would use hand tools to give it its final form as it was being turned on the wheel. By 1903, however, molds had come into use for turning out ceramic pieces commercially, in one operation. These were made of plaster of Paris, gypsum stone from Nova Scotia being about the only kind from which a sufficiently fine plaster could be produced for this particular use.

The designer or modeler of a piece began his work in much the same way that the potter of the old days had set about his, using a potter's wheel practically identical to those used generations before. He designed in clay the vessel he wanted. From this clay model he made a plaster cast, which served as a mold. Vessels could be made from this mold, but to make them in quantity it was necessary to have more than one mold of the same design. However, only one mold could be made from the clay model. A plaster model was needed from which as many plaster molds could be obtained as required. One potter could handle many molds and turn out vessel after vessel, as the molds were whirled about on the swiftly revolving mechanism known as a "jigger," the modern potter's wheel.

A jigger was operated by electric power. It consisted of a base that whirled, as did the old-time whirler that was part of the potter's wheel, but this one whirled with marvelous speed. (The old-time wheel operated by hand or foot power moved much more slowly.) The jigger was equipped with a "pull-down," an upright iron rod to which was attached a shaping tool set to give the exact thickness desired. The potter seized this rod and pulled it down, bringing the tool into the clay and holding it stationary. As the whirler carried the mold about, the clay pressed between the mold and the tool rapidly took shape.

The filled mold was passed into the stove room where, under slight heat, the porous plaster of the mold absorbed moisture from the clay, and the new vessel shrank away from the mold. Removed from the mold, it was given to the "finisher," who smoothed the rough edges and supplied handle, spout, or whatever was required. The new piece was then sent to the "green room," where articles waited to go into the "biscuit" kilns or were left to dry out.

11. A worker removing ware from the molds.

12. An early photograph of a potter smoothing pieces after the firing.

Some pieces could not be put on a jigger but had to be placed on whirlers operated by hand; the clay was then pressed to the mold by means of hand-held tools, as of old. Under this heading came oval dishes, covered dishes, dishes with a footed base, and other departures from regular straight shapes. Another class of hollow ware that did not go to the jigger included chocolate pots, vases, and teapot spouts. These were "cast"—that is, slip that had not gone through the clay press was poured into a mold. Enough of the slip would adhere to the sides of the mold to form the vessel or piece. Rough edges were smoothed off, and then the piece passed on to the green room.

There were fifteen kilns in the Buffalo Pottery. Four of these were biscuit, or bisque, kilns; five were "glost," and six were decorating kilns. The decorating kilns —they looked like vaults—were "muffled" kilns; that is, the kiln proper, or oven, in which the ware was placed for firing on the decorations was built wholly within a firebox. There was open space between the kiln and the firebox, and when the

14. Workers balance on their heads the loaded saggers that must be stacked in the kiln for firing.

13. Early kilns at Buffalo Pottery were coal-fired. Man at upper left is checking to see if the ware is ready.

15. Putting in the last load of ware, before the kiln is sealed and fired.

17. While being fired in the glaze kilns, plates are supported on three points. Afterward, a corps of workers chipped away the three rough spots left by the points.

16. A view of workmen stacking the saggers in a kiln.

fire was built underneath the kiln, the heat could pass around it on all sides.

The bisque and glost kilns were huge round giants (Ill. 16), their conelike tops protruding above the roof of the pottery. These kilns consisted of an outside shell of red brick and cement with a lining of firebrick and fireclay. Each kiln had ten fire holes around the sides of the interior, and from each hole a flue ran to a center hole in the floor, so that the heat was evenly distributed. The kilns were fired by coal that had to be shoveled in by hand.

Thermostats for a kiln were unknown at that time. Instead, to gauge the temperature, the fireman peered through small holes at various points in the kiln walls and observed the condition of heat cones positioned in groups of four. These cones were made of varying proportions of feldspar and clay, of such consistencies that they would melt and droop at different temperatures. When the last little point just bent its head, the fireman knew that then (and not until then) he could stop shoveling on coal (Ill. 13).

The kilns could accommodate thousands of pieces of ware at one time, the bisque kilns burning the clay into ware of the whitest bisque form, the glaze kilns fixing the glaze, or glost. Pieces ready to be fired were put in what were known as "saggers," large coarse earthenware receptacles. (They were made in a special department at Buffalo Pottery.) The saggers were piled in the kiln, one on the other, and the crevices between them sealed with wieners of clay so that no gases, impurities, or dirt of any kind could find way into a sagger. It was a trick of the potters to walk up the steep ladders in the kilns balancing saggers, unsupported, on their heads (Ill. 14) all the way to the very topmost row. Once a kiln was filled with saggers (there were some 1,800 in a firing), the fires were started.

When ware from the green room was taken to the bisque kiln, it was cream-colored and very fragile. After it had been baked for fifty hours at a temperature ranging from 2300 to 2400 degrees Fahrenheit, it emerged pure white in color, hard, and bisquelike. Each piece was then brushed and sandpapered, to make it ready for the next step. Before that step is described, however, a few words should be said about underglaze and overglaze.

Underglaze ware is that on which decorations are applied before the glaze is put on. Because of the intense heat necessary to fix the glaze, decoration requiring the more delicate colors was usually put on later—over the glaze—and then the piece was refired at a comparatively mild heat to fix or set the colors. Ware so decorated is known as overglaze ware; it often boasts especially beautiful artistic effects.

In overglaze ware, Buffalo Pottery equaled all other American potters and excelled many, but it was to the development of a superior underglaze ware that special attention was directed. Until Buffalo Pottery came into that field, with one or two exceptions underglaze ware had never been successfully produced in this country. In almost every instance, American-made underglaze pieces were far inferior to English ones, which were sold here in large quantities. But Buffalo developed underglaze decoration so fine that most imported underglaze ware suffered by comparison. The firm's expert designers stood high in the estimation of the industry. Buffalo Pottery made all its own underglaze colors, and its Designing Department was so well equipped that it could produce colors and designs never attempted before in an American pottery. Underglaze decorations have the advantage of being protected by the glaze—and therefore of not wearing off or being easily damaged.

Ware that was to receive underglaze decoration went directly to the Decorating Department after having emerged from the bisque kiln and been given its brushing and sandpapering. A specially prepared tissue was passed between the copper cylinders of an electric printing machine to be impressed with the design to be used. The imprinted tissue was pressed onto a piece of the ware and rubbed vigorously with a brush so that it would leave behind its sticky ink design. Then the tissue was washed off with soap and water, only the inked design remaining on the piece, which might then be taken to another room to have the coloring done by hand, or lines put on, or a decorative border applied. Or perhaps the piece would be immediately glazed and baked, and additional decoration (if any) added over the glaze.

Design could also be transferred to the unglazed pieces by decalcomania, or the decal process. Pieces so decorated were put first into a kiln for a short time, to dry out the oil of the decal. Then they were dipped in tubs of glaze, to coat them with that preparation, and put into glost kilns at a temperature of 2200 degrees Fahrenheit for twenty-four hours to harden the glaze. When cool, they were ready for shipment.

18. The liner puts simple line decoration on a piece, turning the wheel by hand and applying the color with a brush.

Ware destined to receive overglaze decoration went from the bisque kilns directly to the glaze tubs and then the glost kilns, from which it emerged white and shiny, ready for decoration. Overglaze decorators also used various methods: decalcomania, printing the outlines and filling them in by hand, tinting with colors and various gold treatments, and hand painting. When the decoration was finished, the pieces were fired in the decorating kilns at a temperature of about 1300 degrees. Thence they too went to the ware room, at the extreme end of the building next to the railroad siding, where all finished pieces were packed for shipment.

The production process was a continuous one, with a minimum of lost motion. Although the equipment at Buffalo Pottery was designed for maximum efficiency, probably the most important contributing factor was the skill and experience of the management and the artisans. All their energy and knowledge were directed toward turning out a semivitreous porcelain* that was exclusive in design and pattern. Its quality was much superior to that of the wares produced by competitors, and it was less expensive.

Among the first semivitreous pieces turned out by the new pottery were one-hundred-piece dinner sets in the Modjeska pattern, named for the internationally famous Polish actress. These were given free by the Larkin Company with a twenty-dollar purchase of soap products. A one-hundred-piece Lamare dinner set was given with a sixteen-dollar purchase. Also produced were the fifty-six-piece Modjeska tea set, the fifty-one-piece Modjeska cottage set (a service for six), the sixty-nine-piece Lamare cottage set, and the fifty-six-piece Lamare tea set. A Cairo toilet set consisting of washbowl, pitcher, and ten other pieces was given free with a ten-dollar purchase. The body of this was white, decorated with a cluster of June roses in pink and yellow, with natural green leaves and stems, against a background of brown. The handles and edges were traced in gold. The lustrous glaze finish was guaranteed by the company not to craze.

Advertised as special items at this time were a poppy-decorated chocolate pot and a cracker jar, and a three-piece oatmeal set embellished with roses, lilacs, forget-me-nots, and gold trim. Other special items were a salad bowl decorated with roses and embossed work trimmed in gold and a Canton blue underglaze water pitcher that held three pints. Game, fowl, and fish sets, each consisting of six round plates and an oval platter, were made at this time too. These were produced in both underglaze and overglaze ware. Offered also were a set of six 9-inch historical plates and another ten-piece toilet set in the chrysanthemum pattern with a large cuspidor to match. In addition, there was a series of Doulton-shaped historical and commemorative pitchers and a twenty-two-piece child's tea set in green underglaze decoration. All these were fine pieces, artistic and guaranteed by the pottery not to craze. †

In subsequent years Buffalo Pottery was destined to initiate the manufacture of innumerable fine designs, patterns, and wares. Almost without exception, these

* The early full-size kilns were capable of firing only semivitreous ware. The few pieces of bone china made in the early days were probably fired in a small kiln, perhaps one used largely for experimental or testing purposes. At that time, the terms "semivitreous" and "semiporcelain" were frequently used interchangeably; both referred to a soft-paste, porous material. The longer phrase "semivitreous porcelain" had the same meaning.

† Pieces made by Buffalo Pottery are sometimes found today with various degrees of crazing of the glaze, which could have resulted from any one of several causes, such as putting plates of food in the oven to keep warm. In general, slight crazing does not seriously detract from the value of a piece; of course, crazing so severe as to have permitted discoloration to take place under the glaze is quite another matter—whether it is found on a piece of Buffalo pottery, Staffordshire, or any other ceramic ware.

products are now sought by antique dealers and collectors, and treasured by families who have sentimentally and affectionately kept them a generation and more.

Although most Buffalo wares were manufactured with the Larkin Company in mind, in time they were distributed in wholesale and retail outlets through the country. By 1908, Buffalo Pottery had selling agencies in New York, Chicago, and St. Louis, and by 1911 it was exporting to twenty-seven countries. The first offering of Buffalo Pottery appeared in the Larkin Company catalog of 1904, which explained that whereas it had long been the custom among American potters to "sell seconds for use as premiums," the Larkin Company could "now offer crockery made by Buffalo Pottery, which is of First Quality." (Before Buffalo Pottery was founded, Larkin had imported first-quality Limoges, Dresden, and some English Blue Willow for use as premiums.)

Early Buffalo Pottery pieces can still be found in all parts of the United States today. They can readily be identified, since most of them are clearly marked and dated, bearing the Buffalo Pottery stamp on the bottom. From the beginning, the pottery had the foresight to date almost all the pieces produced, and it continued this policy until complete mechanization entered the picture in the 1940's.

In 1905, an underglaze Blue Willow was produced that was far superior in color, glaze, and body to the imported ware. Buffalo was the first pottery in America to succeed in producing a Blue Willow that not only duplicated but even improved on the underglaze colors of the imported product, and so they were completely justified in claiming to be the "originators of old blue willow in the United States." It was at this time also that a series of advertising and commemorative plates was introduced. These were special orders from business firms, clubs, institutions, and civil organizations.

In 1908, seeking to produce an artistic "quality" product that would compete with—and perhaps be superior to—the prestige pottery imported from England at that time, Buffalo Pottery turned to the production of Deldare Ware. Today, this ware is among the scarcest and most eagerly sought of all Buffalo Pottery products. It commands an extremely high price.

In 1911 and 1912, Buffalo Pottery turned to the manufacture of Abino Ware and Emerald Deldare as well as a host of other products, all of which will be discussed in detail in later chapters of this book.

The change from semivitreous ware to vitrified china occurred in the year 1915. Buffalo Pottery was one of only twelve potteries in the United States where vitreous china was made; over a hundred potteries made semiporcelain, a coarser ware. Thereafter, all pieces of vitrified china manufactured by Buffalo Pottery were stamped "Buffalo China" (Ill. 19) instead of "Buffalo Pottery." However, some pieces of semivitreous ware continued to be made, and these still carried the Buffalo Pottery mark (Ill. 20).

It should be noted here that collectors are mistaken to rate pieces marked "Buffalo Pottery" so much above those marked "Buffalo China." Some of the finest and most artistic work was done on items marked "Buffalo China." The George Washington plate of 1932 is a good example (Ill. 275).

Two years after Buffalo Pottery started making vitrified china, it became apparent that the original facilities were no longer adequate. An enlargement was made consisting of three new buildings with 60,000 square feet of space, two new bisque kilns, and two new glost kilns. This addition gave the pottery a total of 140,000 square feet of working area.

When the United States entered World War I, the military services ordered increasingly large amounts of Buffalo pottery and china. Larkin Company's 1918–1919 fall/winter catalog printed the following announcement, which tells something of the role the pottery played in the war effort, and gives other pertinent information:

ALL BUFFALO POTTERY WARE WITHDRAWN—
GOVERNMENT NEEDS OUTPUT

For more than three years the Buffalo Pottery has been producing vitrified china of which an example is the China Butter Tub and Drainer, offered as a Larkin Product. Some of America's finest deluxe hotels are now equipped with Buffalo Pottery China; 80 American merchant ships are being equipped.

BUFFALO POTTERY CHINA IN U.S. SERVICE

From our entrance into the war, the army and navy have made rapidly increasing demands for Buffalo Pottery China and the war demands of the U.S. Army, Navy, and Hospital service now call for china in unprecedented quantities. Each of the hundreds of the merchant ships now being launched to sail under the American flag will carry real china for its tables. The elimination of semi-porcelain, formerly offered in our catalog, at least for the term of the war, will expedite greatly the production of vitrified china for government use.

ORDERS FILLED WHILE STOCK LASTS

We will fill orders for Buffalo Pottery tea, dinner, and toilet sets offered in our last catalog (No. 79) as long as conditions will permit. To avert disappointment, however, it will be best to order as soon as possible. When we become obliged to decline orders for this ware you may have the satisfaction of knowing that the Buffalo Pottery which for fifteen years has been satisfactorily serving Larkin customers (for which purpose it was built) is now devoted to helping win the war, by furnishing for our soldiers china dishes of a recognized unexcelled quality.

When normal production was resumed at the war's end, a line of dinnerware was made again to be used for premiums as well as sold directly to the public through wholesale and retail outlets. The pottery turned at this time to a much

19.   Some of the trademarks used by Buffalo Pottery on their vitrified ware.

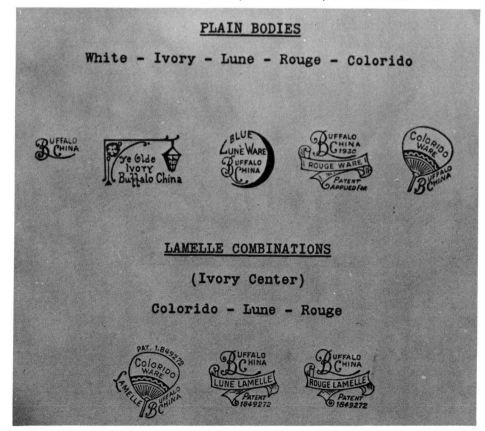

finer and thinner china than they had ever made before. The patterns were called Dresden, Glendale, Blue Bird, and Pink Rose. As part of the effort to regain its prestige, in 1923 the company also went back to producing its highest art line, Deldare Ware. This they continued to turn out until 1925, when high production costs brought the price beyond the average man's means. Thereafter it was discontinued.

An examination of the annual Larkin catalogs indicates that Deldare Ware was offered only once as a premium—in the fall/winter catalog of 1922–1923. That catalog also represented the last time that Buffalo Pottery ware was mentioned as a premium. In the later twenties and in the thirties, the Larkin Company turned almost exclusively to imported china, which was cheaper than producing their own, and Buffalo Pottery turned to the manufacture of exclusive hotel and institutional ware.

Realizing that color was rapidly permeating the entire food industry, the pottery management knew there would soon be a demand for hotel china with solid body color, and they saw to it that experimenting was begun to develop satisfactory body colors. The advantage of dinnerware that is so colored is greater depth and uniformity of color than is possessed by that with color applied only to the surface; and when a solid-body article is chipped, it shows the same color throughout. By 1928, Buffalo's laboratory research had led to the development of the following color line: Ye Olde Ivory, which was ivory color; Lune Ware, which was blue; Rouge Ware, which was pink; Colorido Ware, which was yellow; and Café-au-Lait, which was a deep tan. This new line was use singly or in combinations (Ill. 19).

In 1931, after a great deal of experimentation in the laboratory and factory, Buffalo Pottery perfected a china with an inlaid center of clay, on which it secured a United States Patent. They called this "Lamelle," from the French for lamination. The inlaid center was used in combination with their colored bodies, actually reinforcing the ware and greatly reducing breakage.

Buffalo Pottery was uniquely equipped to produce custom-made hotel ware because of its large and imaginative Art Department. In the following years they produced outstanding, individually designed china for leading hotels, restaurants, railroads, steamship lines, airlines, and other institutions both here and abroad. Although this individualized commercial ware was an artistic success, by the forties it was clear that consolidating the commercial line would be more profitable financially. The company therefore gave up the practice of custom-designing ware, and instead mass-produced a limited number of designs that would be acceptable to many customers.

Some years before this development—in 1936, in fact—illness had forced Louis Bown to resign as vice-president and general manager. His son William, a sales executive, was appointed to succeed him as general manager.

In 1938, the pottery had the fortunate opportunity to hire Robert E. Gould, a man of wide experience in the ceramic industry. A graduate of Ohio State University, Gould had worked for two years as assistant ceramic engineer for R. Thomas Sons Company of Lisbon, Ohio, and for a similar period as chief ceramic engineer for Taylor, Smith & Taylor Company of Chester, West Virginia. In 1929, he had gone to Katowtz, Poland, as general manager of Giesche Porcelain Company, where he remained until 1935, when he returned to the States to become chief ceramic engineer for the Tennessee Valley Authority at Norris, Tennessee. He left that position to join Buffalo Pottery as vice-president, general manager, and a director. (William Bown returned to the Sales Department of the company, where he remained until he resigned in 1941.)

In 1940, it was decided to reorganize Buffalo Pottery. At that time the company name was changed to Buffalo Pottery Incorporated. In 1946, Robert E. Gould was

20. **Buffalo Pottery trademarks.**

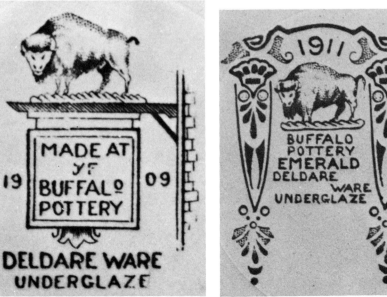

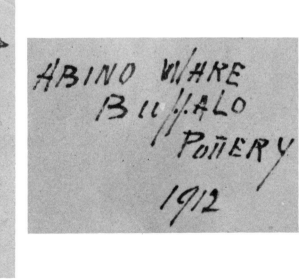

elected president of the company, a position he held until his retirement in 1964, when Harold M. Esty, Jr., was elected to succeed him.

Early in his tenure, Gould realized the need for greater production and consolidation of the Buffalo line, and he began a gradual revamping and modernizing of the plant that included installing the latest in equipment and kilns. Four buildings that were not needed were sold, and the original powerhouse was abandoned; power was purchased from the local utilities. Gould's modernization program eventually resulted in making Buffalo Pottery one of the most efficient and completely automated potteries in the United States.

During World War II, like so many firms, Buffalo Pottery turned its energies into war production. Untold thousands of pieces of decorated ware were made for the Armed Forces.

In 1956, the firm name was once again altered. Recognizing that "Buffalo Pottery" no longer properly identified the company with its product, the board of directors voted that the corporate title be made "Buffalo China, Inc."

Among the artistic accomplishments of Mr. Gould's quarter century as head of Buffalo was the reissuing of the copy of the "Barberini-Portland Vase" that they had first turned out in 1925. This 1946 reissue, also in blue and white, was done by the Lamelle process. He also introduced a series of annual Christmas plates (they were made from 1950 to 1962), in the hope that they would become as popular collectibles as the famous Danish Christmas plates.

Today, Buffalo China, Inc., is mass-producing hotel and institutional ware as fast as production lines will permit. The company has the reputation of being the third largest in this field in the United States. Its present president, Harold Esty, who has been an employee of the company for thirty years, is a grandson of the founder, John D. Larkin.

At the time this book went to press, the Carborundum Company of Niagara Falls, New York, had taken an option on purchasing all the stock of Buffalo China, Inc.

3

Blue Willow and
Gaudy Willow

THE QUALITY OF THE SEMIPORCELAIN BLUE WILLOW PRODUCED BY BUFFALO POTTERY was undoubtedly as good as—and perhaps superior to—that of much of the Blue Willow manufactured by English potteries, with their generations of experience. This pattern with its quaint shapes, stylized decorative devices, and rich blue underglaze color that cannot wear off has as strong an appeal today as it has had for generations. There is no denying the fact that it has been one of the most popular tableware patterns ever made.

Before 1905, American potters had found it impossible to duplicate the rich underglaze cobalt blues and the shadowy blue-whites that distinguished the finest of Blue Willow made elsewhere. In 1905, however, after extensive experimentation, Buffalo Pottery introduced an underglaze Blue Willow that was superior in color, body, and glaze to imported Blue Willow. The firm justly merited the title that it claimed for itself: "The Originators of Semi-Porcelain Blue Willow Pottery in the United States." Their pride in their accomplishment was further indicated by the words (Ill. 23) that were put on the bottom of each piece of Blue Willow dated 1905: "First Old Willow Ware Manufactured in America."

Though the Blue Willow "legend" is reputed to be not a true legend, but only one made up to account for all the various Chinese motifs used in the pattern, many people have considered the tale a charming one, and it has been repeated again and again. Its popularity was such that in the early days the Edison Company, Inc. made a motion picture of it. This opened with the projection onto the screen of a picture of a huge Blue Willow pattern dish. The center of the dish faded out, leaving only the border, which thereafter served to frame the scenes of the story as they unfolded. Another evidence of the popularity of the Blue Willow legend was the fact that at one time the drop curtains of both the Theatre Royal in Greenock, Scotland, and London's Drury Lane pictured a large Blue Willow plate.

According to a Buffalo Pottery leaflet, Blue Willow was mentioned in the original Dr. Syntax verses—the good doctor reminiscing of afternoons long before when he and Cousin Jane drank tea from Old Blue Willow cups on which a youth and maiden stepped lightly over the bridge of love.

In addition to the conventional Blue Willow that Buffalo Pottery so successfully produced over the years and is still making today on vitrified china, the year 1905 saw the firm produce the pattern in hand-decorated colors (Ill. 28). This hand-decorated type has come to be known by collectors as Gaudy Willow. The design is basically the same as on Blue Willow, but a variety of colors are used in the decoration, both over and under the glaze—rust, deep blues, greens, browns, and pure coin gold. Hand-decorated Willow took a great deal longer to produce than the conventional Blue Willow. Consequently, less of it was made, and so today Gaudy Willow is very scarce and also in great demand. Collectors are willing to pay premium prices for it. As far as is known, Buffalo Pottery was the only company ever to produce Gaudy Willow in America. The firm also produced the Willow pattern in a very limited amount in a brown color.

Blue Willow marked "Buffalo Pottery" is more desirable as a collectible than that marked "Buffalo China," and collectors are willing to pay more for the earlier pieces—the earlier the piece, the higher the price—providing the condition is equally fine. Pieces dated 1905 and marked "First Old Willow Ware Manufactured in America" are probably worth the most. However, in general, Blue Willow articles usually sell for more reasonable prices than most other Buffalo Pottery pieces, and so they make a fine specialty for a beginning collector or one on a limited budget.

The Willow "legend" has been printed and reprinted countless times; the version given here is that which appeared in an early booklet put out by Buffalo Pottery. Knowing it will add to any collector's enjoyment of his Blue Willow pieces:

THE LEGEND OF BLUE WILLOW WARE

Once upon a time there was a rich old Mandarin who had an only daughter named Li-Chi. She and her father lived in a beautiful home, two stories in height, a rare thing in China.

If you look at a Willow pattern plate, you will see that not only is the house a two-storied one, but there are outbuildings (to the right) at the back, and large trees, of a rare and costly kind, surrounding it, showing that the owner was a man of great wealth.

Li-Chi was a very pretty girl, and as her father was a rich man, she was always dressed in the softest, brightest silks money could buy.

Her favorite dresses were of peach-colored silk, embroidered with silver, and if you could have seen her sitting on her balcony on a moonlight night, with flowers entwined in her hair, and the shimmering peach-colored silk falling in soft folds about her feet, you would have thought her worthy to marry a prince. But Li-Chi did not want to marry a prince. She had fallen in love with Chang, her father's secretary, who lived in the island cottage you will find at the top of the plate.

The Mandarin was very angry about this, and had forbidden the young man to come to the house, at the same time forbidding Li-Chi to leave it, so that the lovers might have no chance of meeting. He went still further—he betrothed his daughter to a Ta-jin, or Duke, who was rich, but many years older than Li-Chi. Li-Chi had never seen the Ta-jin, but her father came to her one evening as she was sitting on her balcony, which overhung the river, and told her he had made arrangements for her marriage.

"Oh, no! no!" sobbed Li-Chi. "I love Chang! I can not marry anyone else."

"Chang shall never be your husband," replied the Mandarin sternly. "I have promised the Ta-jin that you shall be married to him when the peach tree blossoms."

The willow tree was in blossom then, for it was quite early in the year.

The peach would not bloom until the spring, but every day after this Li-Chi watched the buds of the peach tree, which grew close to her window, unfolding, and she watched them with dread and sorrow in her heart. "Is Chang dead or has he forgotten all about me?" she wondered to herself.

But Chang was not dead, neither had he forgotten; he thought of her night and day, and at last one evening he sent her a message.

She was sitting on her balcony as usual, when a little boat made out of half a coconut shell, and fitted with a tiny sail, floated right to her feet. Inside it she found a colored bead she had given her lover, a sure proof that the boat came from Chang; and also a piece of bamboo paper on which these words were written:

> "When the willow fades away,
>   And the peach tree groweth gay
>   Tell me, sweetheart, can it be
>   They will steal my love from me?"

Li-Chi took her ivory tablets from the bosom of her dress and wrote an answer to his letter in the same strain:

> "When the peach tree blooms, sweetheart,
>   Thou and I must weep and part.
>   Hasten then to take the prize
>   Ere 'tis seen by robber's eyes."

She knew that her lover would understand this flowery language, and she put the tablets in the boat, and lighted a stick of frankincense and placed it in the bow.

And leaning over the balcony, she watched it sail away into the darkness of the night.

"He will come for me before my wedding day," she said softly to herself.

The night air was full of the scent of flowers, and everything was still. Li-Chi half imagined she could hear the blossoms on the willow tree sighing faintly, and saying, "It will be too late—we are dying!" For Chang had promised, the last time they met, that he would come for her while the willow was still in blossom.

And she thought she heard the buds on the peach tree replying: "We are nearly ready to open. Then she will marry the Ta-jin!"

Chang, on the farther bank of the river, waited to draw his frail little bark to land, and when he read the verse on the ivory tablets, his smile went up to the corners of his eyes, as Chinese smiles generally do; and he walked into the gardener's cottage where he was stopping, and called the gardener and his wife.

"Do you know when the Ta-jin is coming?" he said.

"The betrothal feast is fixed for next Thursday, for the moon will then be lucky," replied the old man. "The Mandarin has ordered his gardeners to take six dozen carp out of the fish ponds, and there are to be golden and silver pheasants on the table, and boar's head and roast peacock."

"And six casks of wine to be broached," continued his wife. "And as many oysters as his guests can eat."

"The servants say that the Ta-jin is bringing his bride such a casket of jewels as never was seen," said the gardener. "A necklace of pearls—each pearl as big as a sparrow's egg—"

"Pigeon's egg, stupid!" interrupted the wife.

"Sparrow's egg, imbecile!" he retorted.

"Pigeon's egg, idiot!" repeated the old woman angrily.

"It doesn't matter which," Chang broke in. "What I want to know is whether you could borrow me one of the servants' dresses and smuggle me into the banqueting room that night?"

"It is impossible," replied the gardener, shaking his head.

The old couple knew all about Chang's love story, but they were afraid of helping him. Neither of them dared to risk the displeasure of such a rich and powerful Mandarin as Li-Chi's father.

The next few days passed in preparation for the betrothal feast.

Servants were running hither and thither all the time; the Mandarin never stopped giving orders from morning till night; the banqueting hall was swept and strewn with sweet-scented leaves and the walls and roof hung with colored-silk lanterns and fans.

Everyone was happy and busy except Li-Chi, who sat on her balcony, with her embroidery lying idle on her lap, and her eyes gazing wistfully across the river that separated her from her lover.

On the morning of the betrothal feast the peach tree was covered with lovely pink blossoms, while the willow blossoms hung faded and drooping on the tree.

This made Li-Chi so sad she could not stay on the balcony; she went into her room and sat on a couch, with her head resting on her hands, watching her attendants as they spread out on the floor the rich silk dresses the Ta-jin had sent as a present to his bride.

They were all the colors of the rainbow, pale blue, and pink, and yellow, and purple, embroidered in gold and silver, and one of them was peach-colored silk, embroidered with pearls.

"This is just the dress for a bride," said the women.

But Li-Chi shook her head. "I will not wear peach-color any more," she said.

At noon the Ta-jin sent her by his servant the box of jewels of which the gardener and his wife had spoken. There were diamonds and rubies in it of such size that the Emperor himself would not have despised them. And the necklace of pearls went twice around Li-Chi's neck, and nearly to her waist.

At last her attendants persuaded her to allow them to dress her for her betrothal and they chose a beautiful blue-silk dress, embroidered all over with golden butterflies; because in China butterflies are looked as a symbol of married happiness. And they fastened the pearls around her throat, and put some shining jewels in her hair.

"For she is going to be a great lady—the wife of a duke," they said. "Flowers in the hair are only for common people."

"Now leave me quite alone," commanded Li-Chi, when they had finished.

She was tired of all their foolish talk about the Ta-jin, and wanted to step out once more and see if the willow-blossoms were quite faded, and if there was no message from Chang sailing to her across the water. The women went away, but came back in a moment to tell her that one of the servants wished to speak to her. "Let him come in," said Li-Chi impatiently. The young man who entered wore a long blue cotton robe, and a broad straw hat that half-concealed his face, but as soon as they were alone he took off the hat, making her a low-sweeping bow, and Li-Chi saw that it was Chang himself. For a moment she could not believe it, but when he took her in his arms and kissed her, crumpling up all the golden butterflies in his eagerness, she knew it was really her lover, who had come to save her from marrying the Ta-jin.

"How did you get here?" she asked, sobbing for joy.

"I disguised myself as a beggar," said Chang, showing her the rags he wore under his blue robe. "But when I came to the banqueting room, to ask for alms, everyone was too busy to listen to me. So I managed to slip behind the screen they had spread across the lower end of it and find my way to your room."

"And this?" said Li-Chi, touching his servant's dress.

"One of the servants happened to have left it behind the screen. And now, Li-Chi, how can I disguise you? For we must pass behind the screen again, and through the banqueting-room door into the garden, and across the bridge to the gardener's cottage."

He looked quickly around the room, and found a garment belonging to Li-Chi's old nurse, which covered all her bridal finery, except her pretty little gold-embroidered shoes.

"Never mind my shoes," she said. "I shall run so fast no one will see them."

She took her distaff in her hand because she did not want to be an idle, useless wife to Chang, and she gave him the box of jewels to carry.

I do not think they ought to have taken the jewels, although the Ta-jin had given them to Li-Chi, but perhaps Chang did not know what was in the box, and he was in too great a hurry to ask.

"The willow-blossoms droop upon the bough, my darling! We must delay no longer," he said.

And, indeed, as the lovers crept behind the screen a light breeze shook the last blossoms of the willow to the ground.

"If my father should see us!" whispered Li-Chi, holding her lover's hand very tightly.

"Don't be afraid," said Chang. "I have prayed to the good Genii not to let him catch us. If he comes near they will change us into two stars, shining together, or, perhaps, two turtle doves. You would not mind that, would you?"

"I do not mind anything, except parting from you," replied Li-Chi.

They reached the garden in safety, and Chang led his sweetheart toward the bridge.

But Li-Chi's pretty little shoes would not allow her to run very fast, after all, and when they got to the foot of the bridge, the Mandarin came running down the garden path, with whip in his hand.

"Stop! stop!" he cried furiously. "Will no one stop the thief who has stolen my daughter?"

Chang put Li-Chi in front of him, and she ran across the bridge first, with her distaff, while he followed her with the casket of jewels. Behind them both came the Mandarin, brandishing his whip. But the good Genii, who were watching over the lovers, saw that the Mandarin gained quickly on Chang, and there was no chance of their escaping.

"He will flog Chang to death, and shut Li-Chi up for the rest of her life. What shall we do?" they asked each other.

Then the Genii said, "Let us change them into two turtle doves, that they may be happy together after all." Just as the Mandarin, therefore, put his hand out to seize the young man by the shoulder, the box of jewels fell splash! splash! into the water, and Chang and Li-Chi were changed into two beautiful doves. They at once flew away, out of the Mandarin's reach, and he was left with whip in his hand, and the Ta-jin's jewels at the bottom of the river.

The story does not tell us any more about him—how he got home, or what the Ta-jin said to him when he arrived.

It only tells us that Chang and Li-Chi were as happy as two turtle doves could be.

And the next time you come across a willow-pattern plate, you must look for them, hovering in the air above the bridge.

On the bridge itself you will see three figures, Li-Chi with her distaff, Chang with the jewels, and the Mandarin with his whip.

At one end is the famous willow tree which shed its blossoms the day of the elopement; at the other is the gardener's cottage and at the top of the plate an island, with another on it, in which Chang had hoped to live with Li-Chi.

But instead of that they built a cozy nest in the garden, from which they could watch the willow and the peach tree bloom and fade without any fear of being parted from each other.

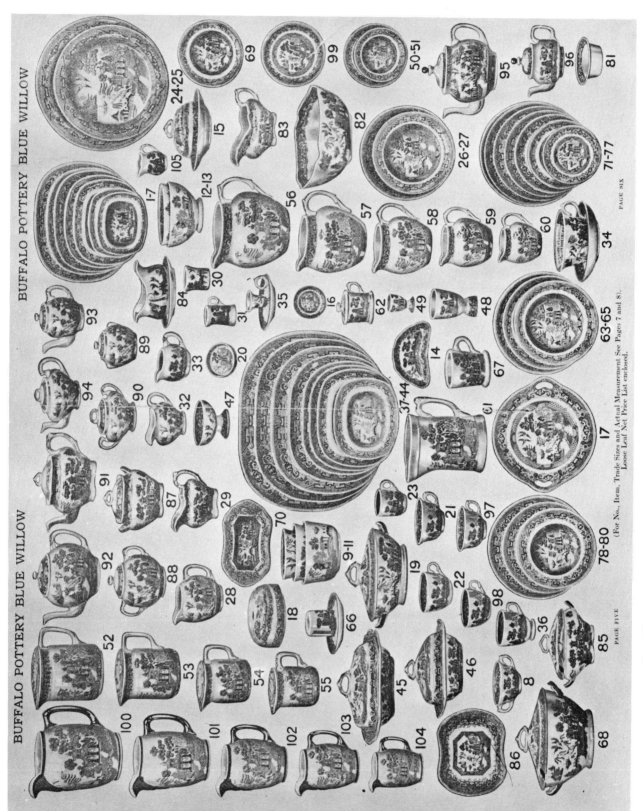

BUFFALO POTTERY BLUE WILLOW

BUFFALO POTTERY BLUE WILLOW

PAGE FIVE

PAGE SIX

(For No., Item, Trade Sizes and Actual Measurement See Pages 7 and 8).
Loose Leaf Net Price List enclosed.

21. The complete line of Blue Willow was illustrated in a 1905 Buffalo Pottery booklet.

SEMI-VITREOUS BUFFALO POTTERY BLUE WILLOW

No.	Items	Trade Sizes	Actual Measurement
1	Bakers	3 inch	5 7/16 inches
2	"	4 "	6 3/16 "
3	"	5 "	7 1/16 "
4	"	6 "	8 1/16 "
5	"	7 "	9 1/16 "
6	"	8 "	10 3/16 "
7	"	9 "	11 1/16 "
8	Bouillons		7 3/4 ounces
9	Bowls	24s	2 pints, 1 ounce
10	"	30s	1 pint, 7 1/2 ounces
11	"	36s	14 ounces
12	" Oyster	30s	1 pint, 10 ounces
13	" "	36s	9 1/2 "
14	Bone Dishes		3 7/8 x 6 7/8
15	Butters, Cov'd		7 3/8 inches
16	Butters, Indv.		
17	Cake Plates		10 1/16
18	Cake Covers		6 5/16
19	Casseroles, Round	7 inch	8 1/16
20	Coasters		3 5/16
21	Coffees, Amoy		10 ounces
22	" Ovide		10 "
23	" A. D		3 1/2
24	Chop Dishes	9 inch	11 1/2 inches
25	"	11 "	13 "
26	Coupes	6 "	7 1/16
27	"	7 "	8 1/16
28	Creams, Round	30s	1 pint, 2
29	" Square	24s	15 ounces
30	" Indv. Double Lip		2 1/16
31	" Tankard No. 1		2 3/8
32	" Macen		8 1/16
33	" Round	48s	2
105	" Toy		1 pint, 5 1/2
34	Coffees, Jumbo		5 1/2 in. x 2 1/4 in.
35	Candle Sticks		
36	Custards, Hld.		7 ounces
37	Dishes	4 inch	3 13/16
38	"	6 "	8 1/16
39	"	7 "	9 11/16
40	"	8 "	10 15/16
41	"	10 "	11 11/16
42	"	12 "	14
43	"	14 "	16
44	"	16 "	18
45	" Cov'd Square	7 "	7 1/2 in. x 9 1/2 in.
46	" "	8 "	8 3/4 in. x 11 1/2 in.
47	Egg Cups, Boston		7 ounces
48	" Double		5 1/2
49	" Single		1 1/2
50	Fruits	4 inch	4 7/8 inches
51	"	4 1/2 "	5 1/4
52	Jugs, Covered	12s	3 pints, 5 1/2 ounces
53	"	24s	2
54	"	30s	1
55	"	36s	1 pint
56	" Buffalo	12s	3 pints, 14 ounces
57	"	24s	2
58	"	30s	2

SEMI-VITREOUS BUFFALO POTTERY BLUE WILLOW

No.	Items	Trade Sizes	Measured up to flange	Actual Measurement
59	Jugs, Buffalo	36s		1 pint, 4 1/2 ounces
60	"	42s		11 1/2 ounces
61	" Hall Boy	24s		3 pints, 6 1/2 ounces
62	Mustards, Covered			5 1/2 ounces
63	Nappies	6 inch		7 7/8 inches
64	"	7 "		8 1/2 "
65	"	8 "		9 3/4 "
66	Match Safes	Rd		6 in. x 2 1/4 in.
67	Mugs			11 ounces
68	Oyster Tureens, Notched Cover	30s		9 3/4 inches
69	Oatmeals			6 1/4 "
70	Pickles, Square			8 1/4 in. x 4 5/16 in.
71	Plates (Ramekin Plate)	3 inch		5 1/4 inches
72	"	4 "		6 1/4 "
73	"	5 "		7 5/16 "
74	"	6 "		8 1/16 "
75	"	7 "		9 1/16 "
76	"	8 "		10 1/16 "
77	"	10 "		10 3/4 "
78	" Deep	5 "		7 1/16 "
79	" "	6 "		8 5/16 "
80	" "	7 "		9 5/16 "
81	Ramekins			3 1/2 ounces
82	Salads, Square	9 inch		9 1/16 in. x 9 5/16 in.
83	Sauceboats, Square			14 1/2 ounces
84	Sauceboats, Fast Stand, Double Handles, Oval			1 pint
85	Sauce Tureen only, Notched Cover			6 1/4 in. x 4 1/2 in.
86	Sauce Tureen Stand only			8 1/4 in. x 6 1/4 in.
87	Sugars Square	30s		2 1/2
88	" Round	30s		2 1/4
89	" Indv. Round	48s		12
90	" Indv. Macen	48s		12
91	Teapots, Square	24s		2 pints, 5 1/2 ounces
92	" Round	24s		3
93	" Indv.	36s		3
94	" Macen	36s		14 ounces
97	Teas, Amoy			1 pint
98	Teas, Ovide			7 ounces
99	Teapots Stands			7 "
100	Jugs, Chicago	12s		6 1/4 inches
101	"	24s		4 pints, 7 ounces
102	"	30s		3
103	"	36s		2 1/2
104	"	42s		1 6 1/4

VITRIFIED BUFFALO CHINA BLUE WILLOW

No.	Items	Trade Sizes	Actual Measurement
95	Teaball Teapots, Vitrified (6 cups)		3 pints
96	" Ind., Vitrified (2 cups)		15 ounces

22. Trade sizes and actual measurements of the Blue Willow pieces from the 1905 booklet.

23. All pieces of Blue Willow made at Buffalo Pottery in 1905 had, on the bottom, the words "First Old Willow Ware Manufactured in America."

24. Close-up of a Blue Willow platter, 16 by 13 inches, dated 1908.

26. The Blue Willow items in this grouping bear various dates. At the top are a demitasse cup and saucer, 9-inch dinner plate, and a teacup and saucer. The bottom row contains two butter pats, sugar bowl, and creamer.

25. Covered vegetable dish with scalloped edge measures 9 by 11 inches. It is dated 1911.

27. Blue Willow of various dates. Top row: a relish dish, 7-inch pitcher, pickle dish; bottom row: compote, egg cup, butter dish.

28. A 10½-inch dinner plate in Gaudy Willow, dated 1907. The design is the same as Blue Willow, but hand-decorated in a variety of vivid colors.

29. Pieces from a child's tea set in Blue Willow. Shown here, in addition to the teapot, open sugar, and creamer, are a luncheon plate, cup and saucer, butter pat, and fruit dish. *Courtesy of Mr. and Mrs. Barry J. Rodgers.*

30. Buffalo China pitchers dated 1922. They measure 10, 8½, and 6 inches respectively (left to right). *Courtesy of Mr. and Mrs. Kenneth E. Francis.*

4

Pitchers and Jugs

AMONG THE MOST COLLECTIBLE OF THE ITEMS MADE AT THE BUFFALO POTTERY WAS a series of pitchers or jugs produced between 1905 and 1909. Most of these were plainly dated on the bottom. It is not known how many were made, but today the demand is great and the supply apparently somewhat limited—a situation that adds to the excitement of collecting.

The shape of some of the pitchers in the series shows a definite English Doulton influence. This is quite understandable—many Buffalo Pottery potters had learned their trade in the English potteries. However, American artistic individualism was not to be denied either, and so the series also boasts pitchers of original design—some tall and thin, others short and squat. (These latter were referred to as "jugs" in the Larkin catalogs.) Some shapes were produced only in these specific years and were never copied thereafter by any other pottery, so far as the authors have been able to learn. These show a good deal of imagination and reflect the influence of the Art Nouveau period at the turn of the century. An excellent example is the pitcher shown in Ill. 45, with its swirling design; the pitcher itself is also shaped along Art Nouveau lines.

The pitcher series had decorations in a wide variety of colors, and in most cases these are as bright and perfect today as when the pitchers were made, because the decorations were applied under the glaze. Some of the designs were transfer-printed on the unglazed pieces, but on many pieces the design was hand-decorated. Quite a number of the pitchers had a line of pure coin gold around the top edge and the handles. Gold was also used in many of the designs.

The jug and pitcher series was made of semivitreous china, since it was produced in the years before the Buffalo Pottery made vitrified ware. The most determined research has failed to reveal any further information about the series. Records are nonexistent; surviving employees cannot recall any details about the ware. Consequently, credit for the designs and decorations cannot be attributed to individual artists. Although the initials of a number of artists appear on the bottom of the various pitchers, none can be linked with a known employee.

The authors' years of research have so far turned up twenty-nine distinctly different specimens in this series. However, new ones continue to show up on the market occasionally, and so the total is quite likely to increase.

Supposedly, the wares of the Buffalo Pottery were to be used as premiums for the Larkin Company, but a search through the Larkin catalogs shows that only eight of the twenty-nine known pitchers ever received a catalog listing. The first was listed in November, 1905; a few subsequent catalogs listed pitchers.

The subjects reproduced on the pitchers covered a relatively wide range—all the way from historical themes, literature, and foreign lands, to flowers, outdoor scenes, and abstract designs (Ill. 35). A list of the known pitchers is given below:

HISTORICAL SUBJECTS

The Landing of Roger Williams	1907
George Washington	1907
The Whaling City—New Bedford, Massachusetts	1907
Pilgrim	1908
John Paul Jones	1907

LITERARY THEMES

Robin Hood	1906
Gloriana	1907 and 1908
Roosevelt Bears	1907
Cinderella	undated
Rip Van Winkle	1907

OUTDOOR SCENES

Sailing Ships and Lightship	1906
The Fox Hunt and the Whirl of the Town	1908
The Old Mill	1907
Wild Ducks	1907
Hounds and Stag	1906
The Buffalo Hunt	undated
The Gunner	undated
Sailors and Lighthouse	1906

DUTCH SCENES

Dutch Jug	1906 and 1907
Holland	1908

OTHERS

Vertical Stripe	1906
Blue Geranium	1905
Triumph (Annual Poppy)	undated
Art Nouveau	1908
Orchids	undated
Chrysanthemum	undated
Mason Jug	1907
Canton Blue Flowers	1905
Melon-shaped China Pitcher	1909

The price for pitchers and jugs varies according to the availability of the particular specimen, and also depends on the demand in the specific area of the country. The usual range in price is from $50.00 to $150, with the trend being steadily upward.

31. Rip Van Winkle jug dated 1906. Height is 6½ inches. Hand-decorated in multicolors. The other side of the jug pictures Rip as a young man, sitting on a log in the forest with his dog and his gun at his side. Under the spout of the jug is a picture of Joseph Jefferson, the actor who played the part of Rip on the stage in 1865 and for years afterward. *Courtesy of Harry H. Larkin, Jr.*

32. Sailor pitcher dated 1906. Height is 9¼ inches. Decoration is in blue. On the opposite side is a lighthouse on a rocky shore. *Courtesy of Mr. and Mrs. Pat Cutini.*

34. Nautical pitcher dated 1906. Height is 9¼ inches. As on the pitcher shown in Ill. 32, the decorations are in blue. The side facing the camera shows a lightship at anchor, positioned to warn ships of treacherous waters. The opposite side has a scene of ships with their sails billowing in the wind. Note the gulls in the border design.

33. Cinderella jug dated 1906. Height is 6 inches. A beautiful jug hand-decorated in a multitude of colors, with a good deal of gold trim. The opposite side pictures the prince trying the slipper on Cinderella's foot. This jug was shown only in the Larkin catalog of 1905, but was also made in subsequent years.

35. A very rare striped pitcher dated 1909. Height is
8 inches. The striped areas are decorated in green, white,
and pink marbleized pattern. The beading and trim were
done in pure gold. *Courtesy of the Vogel family*.

36. Landing of Roger Williams jug, 1906, hand-decorated
in multicolors. Height is 6 inches. This scene shows the
Indians greeting Williams as he landed in Rhode Island.
On the opposite side is Betsy Williams' cottage. The area
below the lip pictures an anchor and capstan (at the center) and Indian tepees. This is one of the few jugs also
made in Deldare.

38. Whaling City jug, souvenir of New Bedford, Massachusetts, 1907. Height is 6 inches. The decoration is in
brown. Scene on the other side shows the *Niger*, last of
the famous full-rigged ships engaged in whaling. In the
area under the spout appears a large wooden fluked
anchor above New Bedford's official seal.

37. Old Mill jug, 1906. Height is 6 inches. The ornate
decoration is blue edged in gold. The same scene appears
on both sides of this jug.

39. The Whirl of the Town and the Foxhunt jug, 1908. Height is 7 inches. The hand decoration in bright colors includes a fox-hunt on the opposite side of the jug. This piece was offered only in the Larkin catalog of 1905, but was also made in subsequent years.

40. Pilgrim pitcher, 1908. Height is 9 inches. Hand decoration is in bright colors. Miles Standish appears on the side shown. The main picture on the opposite side is of John Alden and Priscilla, but there are other smaller scenes too. Under the spout appears: "The spinner, the queen of Helvetia." Mrs. Walter Robb of Buffalo, New York, the daughter of John D. Larkin, owns this pitcher in Deldare, also dated 1908.

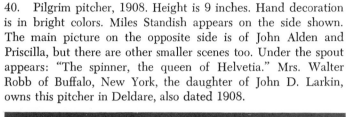

41. Robin Hood jug, 1906. Height is 8¼ inches. Hand-decorated in rich colors. The opposite side shows Robin Hood shooting an arrow into a poacher who had killed a deer. This jug was offered in the Larkin catalog of 1905. It was made also in a Deldare body, dated 1906.

42.   Roosevelt Bears pitcher. The years 1906 and 1908 both appear on the bottom of
this pitcher. Height is 8 inches. Hand-decorated in a host of bright colors, the pitcher is
covered with scenes and quotations from *The Roosevelt Bears,* a series of children's
books written by Seymour Eaton and illustrated by Floyd Campbell.

43. George Washington jug, 1907. Height is 7½ inches. Jug has blue decoration, gold trim. Washington's home at Mount Vernon appears on the opposite side. There is a full portrait of Washington under the spout. This jug was offered only in the Larkin catalog of 1905.

44. Gloriana pitcher, 1907. Height is 9¼ inches. The pitcher is exquisitely hand-decorated in many colors, with gold trim used lavishly. (The same pitcher was made also with blue decoration.) On the opposite side, Gloriana appears in a different setting, wearing a morning glory for a bonnet. Gloriana was the name Spenser used (in his *Faerie Queene*) for Elizabeth I.

45. Art Nouveau pitcher, 1908. Height is 8½ inches. Hand-decorated in blue and gold. The flowers bear some resemblance to the Mayapple or mandrake.

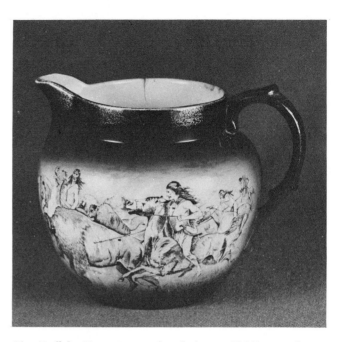

46. Holland jug, dated both 1906, 1908. Height is 6 inches. Colorful hand decoration includes three scenes of Dutch children around the body of the jug and a rural landscape around the top.

47. Buffalo Hunt jug, undated (circa 1906). Height is 6 inches. Top border and handle are dark blue-green surmounted with a band of gold. The scene is adapted from Frederick Remington's painting "Her Calf" (1897); a bison calf appears on the other side of the jug. A version of the same hunting scene appears on two of the platters pictured in the next chapter.

48. Wild Ducks jug, 1907. Height is 6 inches. Again, dark blue-green decor with gold band around the top. The wild-ducks scene is the same as appears on one of the plates in Ill. 65 (if some allowance is made for the distortion caused by the curve of the jug). Pictured on the other side of the jug is a dog named "Major, Old Hoss" that is believed to have belonged to William Rea, the first superintendent of the pottery.

49. Hounds and Stag jug, 1906. Height is 6½ inches. Hand decoration includes a continuous multicolor scene around the top showing hounds harrying stags. Flowers resembling geraniums and thistles decorate the lower part of the jug. Buffalo Pottery artists took quite a few liberties in interpreting the flower species used on jugs and pitchers.

50. Dutch jug, 1907. Height is 6½ inches. This piece is hand-decorated in a variety of vivid colors. The scene on the other side includes a windmill.

51. Triumph jug, undated (circa 1906). Height is 7 inches. Blue annual poppies circle the jug. Gold is also used in the design.

52. Geranium jug, 1905. Height is 6½ inches. All-over blue-and-white decoration on this jug consists of geraniums and their leaves. The geranium jug was listed in Larkin catalogs from 1905 to 1910. It was also made with multicolor decoration.

53. Orchid Spray jug, circa 1905. Decoration on the white body consists of orchid sprays in pastel shades.

54. Mason jug, 1907. Height is 8¼ inches. Decoration in shadings of deep blue-green consists of what appear to be Neapolitan fishermen and Roman ruins around the top and a relatively conventional fruit and flower design around the lower part.

55. Jug with "The Gunner" scene (which also appears on the plate in Ill. 70) dates from about 1905. Height is 6 inches. Decoration is deep blue-green in color against a white background. Top border is speckled with gold.

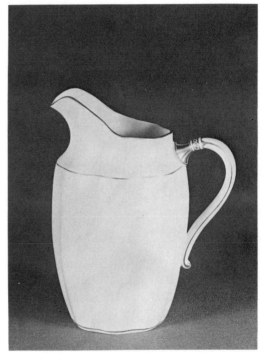

56. John Paul Jones pitcher, dated 1907. Height is 9¼ inches. Blue decoration includes a battle scene on the reverse side in which Jones's ship, *Bon Homme Richard*, and the [Se]*Rapis* are engaged in a fierce struggle.

57. Melon-shaped pitcher, 1909. Height is 8¾ inches. This graceful pitcher with its restrained decoration in gold is made of bone china. A number like it were made for Mrs. John D. Larkin, who gave many away as gifts.

5

Fish, Fowl, and
Deer Sets

THE FISH, FOWL, AND DEER SETS PRODUCED BY BUFFALO POTTERY IN THE EARLY
years were extensively used by the Larkin Company as premiums. The fact that
the sets were advertised continuously in the catalogs for so many years not only
attests to their great popularity but also helps to explain the wide distribution
they achieved. A complete set in any of these patterns consisted of an oval serving
platter 15 inches by 11 inches and six 9-inch plates.

The fowl or bird set appeared in the Larkin catalog from 1908 through 1909.
The deer-family set was listed from 1909 through 1914; the fish set from 1909
through 1910. Although the 1907 catalog did not list any game sets, the authors
have found pieces bearing that date—for example, fowl plates. Perhaps these were
produced in advance, anticipating a catalog listing the following year.

The Larkin catalogs of 1905 through 1910 showed an attractive pair of 9-inch
game plaques ("placques" in the catalogs) decorated under the glaze in deep
blue-green, with a scalloped edge rimmed in gold. One plaque was entitled "The
Gunner" (Ill. 70); the other was "Wild Ducks" (Ill. 65). A plate showing wild
ducks was also part of the fowl set. The plaques, which could be obtained
singly or as a pair, were drilled on the back for hanging. They too were popular
and widely distributed.

Very scarce, and probably done only in limited numbers for other customers of
the pottery rather than the Larkin Company, were various game and sporting
plates with hand-painted decoration, like those shown in Ills. 71 to 78. These were
individually designed, the subjects apparently chosen according to the preference
of the customer or the whim of the artist. They should not be confused with the
wildlife sets described below.

The year of manufacture appears on the reverse side of most fowl sets, but
unfortunately the pottery neglected to date both the deer and fish sets. Also
unlike the deer and fish sets, each piece in the fowl set has the name of the
species under its picture. All three types of sets were made of semivitreous china,
as were all the individual wildlife plates except the one shown in Ill. 78.

Fish Sets (Ills. 58–61)

Native American game fish, both fresh- and salt-water varieties, were utilized for the action scenes displayed on these plates. R. K. Beck, the famous wildlife painter, created the scenes, which were applied by decal under the glaze and were faithful to the original Beck paintings. His name appears on every plate. The borders are usually myrtle green or deep blue-green, edged in pure gold; the centers are white. Some sets, however, were made with a white border edged in gold. The fish and their background appear in natural colors.

Fowl or Bird Sets (Ills. 62–65)

The original drawings of the American game birds portrayed on the fowl sets are generally attributed to the Buffalo Pottery artist Ralph Stuart, although his signature cannot be found on any of the pieces. Each scene is extremely well executed, with the birds shown in great detail. The scenes were applied by transfer print, under the glaze, in various shades of blue-green. The edges are scalloped, most of them being trimmed in gold; the borders are also deep blue-green. An embossed scroll-type design was used on many of the pieces, but not on all of them. However, as is true in the case of the deer and fish series as well, the background colors were not always consistent; and some fowl plates also have a different style of border—light green shading into white, the gold-trimmed edge smooth instead of scalloped.

The large oval platter in the fowl set (Ill. 62) was unique in that the game bird continuity was not adhered to—on this platter was a version of Frederick Remington's renowned 1897 painting "Her Calf."

Deer Sets (Ills. 66–69)

Each plate in the deer set pictured a different species of deer in its natural habitat, and on each piece both a male and female of the species were portrayed. R. K. Beck also created these scenes, which (like those on the fish sets) were applied by decal under the glaze. The deer scenes were equally faithful to the original Beck paintings. Again, Beck's signature appears near the bottom of each scene.

The borders on these sets were done in myrtle green edged in pure gold; the centers were white. Natural outdoor colors were used for the game and the background. The background color scheme was not always adhered to, however, and many of the sets had a border of darker green defined between two bands of gold, though the centers of the plates were the same. Other border variations are also found.

Today, Buffalo Pottery collectors sometimes hang one or more of these colorful sets on the walls of a den or game room. An attractive decoration, they are most particularly prized by sportsmen because they so accurately depict wildlife in its natural environment.

Fortunately, such sets are not as yet too difficult to obtain, and with some effort a collector can complete the set of his preference within a reasonable time. Currently, the 9-inch plates can usually be found for from $15.00 to $25.00 each, and the platters for about $35.00. Of course, the collector lucky enough to find a complete set in perfect condition can expect to pay a premium price for it. The individual game and sporting plates are so seldom seen on the market that it is difficult to suggest a reliable price range. Certainly, any one would sell for much more than any single plate or platter from the wildlife sets.

58. The fish-set platter, 15 by 11 inches. This was shown in the Larkin catalogs of 1909 and 1910. Like the six fish plates that accompany it, it is decorated in natural colors and signed "R. K. Beck." The species shown on the platter is a smallmouth black bass.

59. The plates in the fish set measure 9 inches in diameter. The one at the left pictures a landlocked salmon; the one at the right, a rainbow trout.

60. A striped bass is shown on the plate at the left, a cutthroat trout on the one at right.

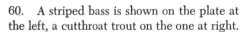

61. Fish-set plates showing the Atlantic salmon (at left) and the Great Northern pike.

62. Oval platter, 15 by 11 inches, is decorated with a buffalo-hunting scene adapted from Frederick Remington's painting "Her Calf" (1897). Oddly, though animals are featured in the scene on the platter, the six plates in the set show wild game birds. Borders are deep blue-green. This set was shown in the Larkin catalogs of 1903 to 1909, though some pieces bear a 1907 date.

63. Two of the plates from the fowl set. The one at left, dated 1908, pictures mallard ducks; the one at right, dated 1907, the American herring gull.

64. The 1908 game plate at left shows dusky grouse; the 1907 plate at right, a wild turkey. On all the plates of the fowl set, the name of the bird appears in small letters at the bottom, close to the border.

65. An American woodcock appears on the 1907 plate at left. The plate at right, dated 1908, shows wild ducks.

66. The deer set, like the fish set, was decorated with scenes taken from original paintings by R. K. Beck. The oval platter, 15 by 11 inches, shows white-tailed deer against a multicolor natural background. All pieces of the set are signed by Beck but none are dated. They were listed in the Larkin catalogs from 1909 to 1914.

67. Two plates from the deer set showing moose (at left) and eastern white-tailed deer.

68. The plate at the left shows elk; the one at right, sika deer.

69. The plate at the left shows fallow deer; the plate at right, caribou deer.

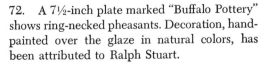

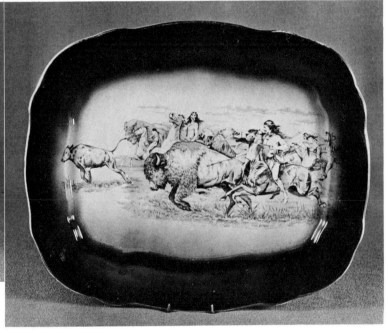

70. Plaque measuring 9 inches, titled "The Gunner," is dated 1907. Decoration is in deep blue-green, under the glaze. Edge is trimmed in gold. Plaque with this decoration was shown in Larkin catalogs from 1905 to 1910.

71. Rectangular platter, 11 by 14 inches, has a deep blue-green border. Edge is scalloped and rimmed with gold.

72. A 7½-inch plate marked "Buffalo Pottery" shows ring-necked pheasants. Decoration, hand-painted over the glaze in natural colors, has been attributed to Ralph Stuart.

73. A 9½-inch plate bearing the legend "Champion—Bromley Crib." The plate is not dated. Persistent research turned up the information that the bulldog Bromley Crib was registered with the Kennel Club in London, England, in 1897, his owner being one H. A. Marfleet, Esq., also of London. But no information has come to light about the client for whom the plate was made, or the purpose. *Courtesy of Alice Herrmann Antiques.*

74. Ralph Stuart again chose ring-necked pheasant for his subject on this 10½-inch, signed but undated plate. The decoration is hand-painted under the glaze. *Courtesy of Mrs. Fred Meatyard.*

75. Though the artist's name does not appear on this undated 9-inch plate, the scene showing a crane is hand-painted under the glaze. Border design is in black. *Courtesy of the Vogel family.*

76. Handsome 9-inch plate signed "R. Stuart" and dated 1916. Decoration is hand-painted under the glaze against an ivory background. *Courtesy of the Vogel family.*

78. An 8½-inch plate, signed "R. Stuart," bears a scene depicting quail, hand-painted over the glaze. The ornate border decoration is in gold. Reverse side carries the words "First Thin China made at Buffalo Pottery, August, 1915." *Courtesy of the Vogel family.*

77. Peacock and vine are hand-painted on a white background, under the glaze. Plate measures 9 inches in diameter. *Courtesy of the Vogel family.*

6

Historical Plates and Commemorative and Advertising Wares

THIS CHAPTER MUST NECESSARILY BE DIVIDED INTO TWO DISTINCT CATEGORIES, THE first (and earliest) being the historical plate series, and the second the various commemorative and advertising items. Although these two series were produced at approximately the same period of time, they were for the most part diverse in shape, color,* and design, and made for different purposes.

Historical Series (Ills. 79–84)

This series was first offered as a premium in the Larkin catalog of January, 1905. It was shown continuously thereafter until the catalog of 1910. A complete set of historical plates, available in either Canton blue or green, consisted of six 10-inch round plates, each one different, showing a site made famous in the early history of the country. The exception, not a historic site, was the early view of Niagara Falls, surely as famous as most historic buildings. (This same view of Niagara Falls was used to decorate a 7½-inch plate—either in deep blue-green or multicolor.)

The scenes on the historical series were reproduced from fine steel engravings, and are exact in every detail. Unfortunately, no specific engraver can be credited. The edges of the plates are very slightly scalloped; the borders—well executed—combine a geometric pattern and floral clusters. The plates are semivitreous china.

The reverse side of each plate is clearly marked "Buffalo Pottery Underglaze," but this series does not bear the date of manufacture. One innovation in the trademark on these plates is the use of an eagle instead of the usual buffalo. The title of the scene and its location are given beneath the trademark in each case. The White House plate carries a partial history of the house on the reverse side.

The majority of the pieces from this series that the authors have seen have survived the years extremely well. Obviously, thousands of sets were distributed

---

* The color used on many of the pieces referred to in this chapter was described in Larkin catalogs as being "robin egg blue." Since the actual color is a deeper blue-green than what is generally regarded today as robin's-egg blue, in their text the authors have termed the color "deep blue-green," to avoid misleading or confusing beginning collectors.

to Larkin customers, and although they are not available in great supply today in antique shops, the price is relatively moderate. At a recent auction, a complete set of six plates was sold for $75.00.

Commemorative and Advertising Pieces (Ills. 85–113)

Early in this century it was quite common for merchants, religious institutions, fraternal organizations, and civic groups to distribute china items free, as a gesture of goodwill. Some of these items openly advertised a business establishment. Some were decorated to commemorate a building, place, or organization, and these too may have been given away by commercial firms, even though they bore no advertiser's name. During most of the years Buffalo Pottery was in operation, the fad of collecting souvenirs was also in its heyday; hence, it is possible that some of the plates the firm made and decorated with buildings and the like may have been made for the souvenir market. In any case, it is known that the firm realized the potential of the commemorative and advertising market, and having the facilities to manufacture appropriate items, solicited this type of business from all parts of the country.

No records remain of the various items the pottery made for this market, and none of these wares were ever listed in any Larkin catalog. The authors have discovered twenty-six deep blue-green plates of various kinds. Here again, additional plates may well turn up. Most of the designs and pictures used on these plates were specially drawn by Buffalo Pottery artists to meet the requirements of individual purchasers. A few customers elected to have the scenes shown on the existing historical series reproduced for their needs.

Not all commemorative and advertising pieces were dated. The earliest date found on plates is 1905; the latest, 1911. Apparently the plates were discontinued in that year. The Buffalo Pottery trademark appears clearly on the back of all the plates, and on some, historical or other pertinent information can also be found on the reverse side. All the scenes were put on under the glaze.

These plates are approximately 7½ inches in diameter, with the exception of the Teddy Roosevelt plate (Ill. 87), which measures 8 inches. Another distinctive feature of that plate is its outer border, which is decorated in the Bonrea pattern with deep blue-green and gold. The majority of the plates have a deep blue-green border shading into a white center; most of the scenes are also done in deep blue-green. A few pieces, such as the Improved Order of the Red Men plate (Ill. 90), and those picturing Mt. Vernon (Ill. 95) and Niagara Falls (not shown), were hand-decorated in several colors, as well as being available entirely in deep blue-green. The scalloped edges were trimmed in pure coin gold. It is believed that, in a number of cases, more than one customer elected to use the same design. The advertising plates were also semivitreous china decorated under the glaze. In most instances, like the plates in the historical series, they remain in extremely good condition today and show few age checks and little discoloration.

Not pictured in this book are three additional advertising plates that the authors learned of quite recently. One—7½ inches in diameter and dark blue-green in color—shows a smelter and a smokestack, identified on the plate as B. & M. SMELTER, AND THE LARGEST SMOKE STACK IN THE WORLD. 506 FT. HIGH. GREAT FALLS, MONTANA. Another plate of the same size and color shows the McKinley Monument in Buffalo. The third plate, also 7½ inches, has multicolor decal decoration on a white body. On the front are Generals Wolfe and Montcalm, with a monument between them reading: "Here died Wolfe victorious./ Ter Centenary/ 1759 Quebec 1908." The border pictures all the Canadian provincial crests. The back of this plate is marked "Registered 1908/ W. A. Reynolds."

Entirely different in color and size are three other plates that have come to the authors' attention. Deep blue and white in color, they resemble the English commemorative plates put out by Rowland & Marcellus. The first two measure 10½ inches in diameter; the third is only 9½ inches in diameter. The first, dated 1908, commemorates New Bedford, Massachusetts (Ill. 85); the second, a plate for the General A. P. Stewart Chapter, United Daughters of the Confederacy, Richmond, Virginia (Ill. 86A), is undated. The third and smallest, also undated, was made for the Women's Christian Temperance Union (86B). No doubt more plates of this type will come to light.

For customers who did not want to advertise or to commemorate an event with a plate, the pottery could provide mugs. These were approximately 4 inches high (Ills. 109–113). Although the background colors of the mugs varied widely, all mugs were shaped alike.

The wares described in this chapter are becoming increasingly popular with collectors. The plates, easy to display to good effect, generally attract favorable comment; some are real conversation pieces. Prices range from $18.00 up, the multicolored ones bringing the higher figures. The Teddy Roosevelt plate doubtless brings the highest price of all because it is extremely rare. Mugs sell for approximately $12.00 or higher.

79.· The plates in this and the five immediately following photographs make up the historical series offered in Larkin catalogs from 1905 until 1910. The decoration on these 10-inch plates is done in Canton blue or green, under the glaze; pieces are not dated but each one is described on the back. The familiar Capitol building in Washington appears on this one.

80.   On the reverse of this plate is the following legend: "The White House, Washington. Erected 1792. 1st occupied by John Adams. Partially destroyed 1814. Restoration 1816."

81. The Niagara Falls plate.

82. Plate showing Independence Hall in Philadelphia.

83. Washington's home, Mount Vernon, appears on this plate of the historical series.

84. The sixth plate in the historical series. On the back is the following: "Faneuil Hall Boston/ Cradle of Liberty, 1742."

85. Commemorative plate, 10½ inches in diameter, made for the city of New Bedford, Massachusetts. Plate is decorated in blue, under the glaze, and is dated 1908. Below the scene, on the front, are the words "New Bedford Fifty Years Ago / original painting by William A. Wall in 1857."

86 A. The 10½-inch plate, also decorated in blue under the glaze, that was produced around 1908 in commemoration of the General A. P. Stewart Chapter, United Daughters of the Confederacy, No. 81, of Richmond, Virginia.

86 B. Commemorative plate (9 inches), with deep blue underglaze decoration was made for the Woman's Christian Temperance Union (W.C.T.U.) circa 1908. On back are these words: "Souvenir Plate of the World's and National W.C.T.U. and the Crusade. Designed by Mrs. Anna Onslatt, Coryden, Ind." The border is decorated with the homes of the leaders in this movement in its early days, and a church that was involved in it also. In the center is the home of Frances E. Willard, second president of the national organization (1879–1898). *Courtesy of Pinneys' Antiques.*

87. Commemorative plate showing Theodore Roosevelt. This 8-inch plate, dated 1905 and marked "Buffalo Pottery China," is decorated under the glaze in deep blue-green with gold tracings. The border is in the Bonrea pattern.

88. Commemorative plate titled "Buffalo, N.Y.," decorated in underglaze dark blue, is 7½ inches across. Border here is also in the Bonrea pattern. Buffalo Pottery commemorative and advertising plates range in date of manufacture from 1905 to 1915.

89. A 7½-inch commemorative plate. This one shows the Hudson Terminal Buildings in New York City. It is decorated in deep blue-green under the glaze.

90. Made for the Improved Order of the Red Men, this 7½-inch commemorative plate is one of the few that came hand-decorated in multicolors also.

91. A 7½-inch commemorative plate made for the Erie Tribe of the Improved Order of the Red Men.

92. On the back of this 7½-inch commemorative plate decorated in deep blue-green are the words "Held at Buffalo June 18–24, 1911." Plate was made for the Modern Woodmen of America.

93. Deep blue-green commemorative plate (7½ inches) made for the Benevolent and Protective Order of Elks in honor of their dead brothers.

94. A 7½-inch commemorative plate made for Trinity Church, New York City, about 1906. Decoration is in deep blue-green.

95.   Commemorative plate, 7½ inches in diameter and titled "Washington's Home at Mt. Vernon," came in hand-decorated multicolor as well as deep blue-green.

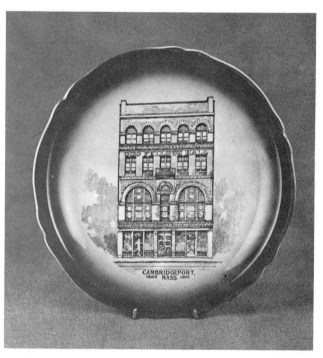

96.   Commemorative plate showing the Odd Fellows Hall in Cambridgeport, Massachusetts (1884–1910), is made in the usual size and deep blue-green color.

97.   Deep blue-green, 7½-inch commemorative plate showing Gates Circle, Buffalo, N.Y., circa 1907.

98.   This 7½-inch, deep blue-green commemorative plate was made for St. Mary Magdalen Church, Buffalo, N.Y. On the reverse side is the caption "First mass said cor. Fillmore and E. Utica, June 25, 1890. First mass said in school building, March 18, 1900. The dedication of the new church, Oct. 20, 1907."

99. Commemorative plate, decorated in the usual deep blue-green, showing the White House, Washington, D.C. Back is labeled with the name of the structure, and adds, "erected 1792."

100. Commemorative plate, circa 1906, of the usual size and deep blue-green color, bears the following legend on the reverse: "Faneuil Hall, Boston, Mass. Cradle of Liberty, 1742."

101. Commemorative plates decorated with portraits of George and Martha Washington. Plates measure 7½ inches and are deep blue-green in color of decoration. *Courtesy of Frances Bryan Murray.*

102. Advertising plate, 7½ inches in diameter, made for L. L. Millring. Like most of the commemorative plates, advertising plates were decorated under the glaze in deep blue-green.

103. This advertising plate, labeled "Main St." and made around 1905, was produced for the second birthday of the Sweeney Company, Buffalo, N.Y., whose store sign is among those that can be seen on it.

104. An undated advertising plate, 7½ inches and decorated in the usual deep blue-green, is marked on the reverse: "Compliments of 'The Home Furniture and Carpet Co.' / 412 & 414 Summit Street / Toledo, Ohio."

105. Made for Bing and Nathan, Buffalo, N.Y., this 7½-inch, deep blue-green advertising plate reads on the reverse: "Builders of happy homes, a dollar or two will do."

106.   A 7½-inch advertising plate showing Independence Hall, Philadelphia, Penn., was made for Katzmann's Store in Springville, N.Y., April 1, 1907.

107.   This advertising plate is clearly marked "The Locks, Lockport, N.Y." The reverse side reads: "Old Home Week, July 24–30, 1910. Compliments of Beirlt Bros. 'Complete Home Furnishers.'"

108. A scene showing Jack Knife Bridge, Buffalo, N.Y., decorates advertising plate that reads on the reverse: "Compliments of George Krug, Sample Room, 592 William St., Buffalo, N.Y."

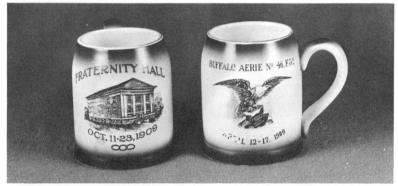

109. Commemorative mugs, both 4½ inches tall. The one at left was made for the Independent Order of Odd Fellows; the one at right for Fraternal Order of Eagles. Decoration on mugs was always multicolor.

110. Three advertising mugs, all 4½ inches tall. The one in the center, made for the Masonic order, is white with blue decoration. The Buffalo Club mug at left has gold lettering on a yellow background. The Bing and Nathan mug is lettered in black on a brown body, and bears a colorful picture of a friar on the reverse side.

111. A commemorative mug made for the Calumet Club of Buffalo, January 26, 1915. Decoration is black lettering against blue and gold.

112. Made for Beechland Farms, this 3½-inch mug has brown decoration on a white background.

113. A 4½-inch mug with decoration in green and brown against a white background. It is captioned "F.C. Orioles, #1 — Broadway Auditorium — April 16–27th, 1913." *Courtesy of Mr. and Mrs. A. Siepierski.*

7

Deldare Ware

CONNOISSEURS OF BUFFALO POTTERY READILY AGREE THAT THE MOST ARTISTIC pieces produced by the firm were Deldare Ware. Today, these are not only jealously cherished and eagerly sought for their originality of design but also for their striking colors.

The origin and development of Deldare can be directly attributed to three men, all now deceased—Louis Bown, William Rea, and Ralph Stuart. Bown, the first general manager and vice-president of the pottery, dreamed of an art pottery that would lend prestige to the company and also compete with the fine products of the English Staffordshire factories. Rea, a ceramic engineer and the first superintendent of the pottery, was responsible for developing the Deldare body. Although the body color was not called Deldare until 1908, Rea apparently had been experimenting with the formula in earlier years. To achieve the distinctive olive-green color, he devised a mixture whose main ingredients were English Ball Clay and Tennessee Ball Clay, to which a certain percentage of oxide of chrome was added. English Ball Clay was used in this formula because of its natural color characteristic.

The authors have found Robin Hood (Ill. 41), the Landing of William Rogers (Ill. 36), and Pilgrim (Ill. 40) pitchers in the Deldare body color dated 1906 and 1907. Although these pieces are not marked "Deldare," there is no question but that they were made from the Deldare formula; the color is identical. The decorative figures and scenes are outlined in black, but not filled in with the colors so characteristic of Deldare. These pitchers are good evidence that Rea had developed the Deldare body before 1908. It should be noted here that the term "Deldare" pertains only to the solid body color of this ware, regardless of the subject matter of the decoration. If chipped, a piece of Deldare appears the same color throughout.

Cooperating with Rea in his quest for the Deldare body formula was George H. Wood, who was superintendent of the clay shop at that time. Rea had brought him from the Crescent Pottery in Trenton, New Jersey, in July, 1903. First employed as a turner, Wood showed such ability and knowledge of chemistry that he was rapidly advanced to the position of superintendent of the clay shop. A man of numerous and diverse talents, in addition to being a potter and chemist he was a chiropractor, musician, artist, author, and photographer. Wood retired from the pottery at the same time as Rea, in 1927.

76

The decorative scenes used on Deldare—Fallowfield Hunt scenes, for example —appeared also years later (in the 1930's) on Colorido, Lune, Rouge, Café au Lait, and Ye Old Ivory china. They were done in full color exactly as on Deldare Ware, but these pieces are not, and should not be represented as, Deldare. They are extremely attractive, nonetheless, and are regarded as choice items by collectors. They are also very scarce.

The choice of these scenes used to decorate Deldare and the original drawing of them was largely the work of Ralph Stuart. In a telephone interview, Mrs. Stuart told the authors of the many nights her husband and Bown and Rea spent at the Buffalo Public Library, poring endlessly over books to find suitable subjects that could be adapted for use on Deldare. Stuart doubtless needed the technical expertise of the others to aid him in his choices. (Incidentally, Ralph Stuart's, as well as his wife's, signature can be found on many pieces of Deldare.)

The greatest disappointment the authors suffered in their research was the failure to discover proof of the origin of the word "Deldare." Various ideas as to the origin of the name have been suggested, but no substantiating evidence has ever turned up. Dee Albert Gernet, in *Spinning Wheel Magazine*, March, 1963, suggested that the name Deldare was derived from famous English decorative lines such as Denholm, Devereaux, and Doulton. Another theory is that Deldare was derived from Della, the name of a daughter of an executive of the pottery. Still another suggestion is that it was taken from the name of a street in Buffalo, Delaware Avenue, which at that period was the most exclusive street in the city. A fourth theory holds that the name was chosen because the originators considered the ware delicate, and therefore coined the word Deldare from "delicate."

Recently, we had the pleasure of interviewing Mr. and Mrs. Franz Bach of Amherst, New York. Mr. Bach, now retired, was manager of the Park Country Club of Amherst, which used Buffalo Pottery products. For a housewarming gift in 1941, Louis Bown invited the Bachs to select Deldare from ware that the pottery had on display. The Bachs questioned him about the origin of the name, and Mrs. Bach clearly remembers his reply, which was as follows: "My wife and I were vacationing at a resort in the Delaware Water Gap in about 1907, and while standing on the porch, looking down the picturesque Delaware River, I was so awed with its beauty that an inspiration came to me to name the new olive-green ware Deldare, after the Delaware Water Gap."

Before Mrs. Stuart died, she too expressed a belief that the word was derived from "Delaware," but she thought it was the state of Delaware from which "Deldare" came. Perhaps the Delaware derivation is the true one. However, some of the other suggestions also have a degree of plausibility and, after all, the complete and authentic story apparently was known only to the three originators of the ware, and is now buried with them.

The bulk of the early Deldare was made in the years 1908 and 1909, only one design of Deldare being made in 1910. This was the 1910 calendar plate (Ill. 234), of which an extremely small quantity was made. Today it is considered a choice collector's item and sells for upward of $200. All the early Deldare is plainly marked with the Deldare trademark, and most pieces are also dated with the year of manufacture.

A completely new and different type of Deldare was introduced in 1911. This series is perhaps the finest and most sought-after of all the Deldare produced at the pottery, and it commands the highest prices. It was known as "Emerald Deldare" (Ills. 179–222), and virtually every piece is dated that year, 1911. This Deldare is in very short supply. Anyone possessing a piece of the distinctive ware is most fortunate. Deldare was discontinued at the end of 1911, except for a few experimental pieces and special orders, and not reissued for a dozen years.

As mentioned earlier, during World War I the pottery produced ware exclusively for the Armed Forces. After the war, management was anxious for the firm to regain its former prestige, and so Deldare production was resumed in 1923, 1924, and 1925. Then production was discontinued once more. The cost of manufacture had become exorbitant. Deldare was never produced again after 1925.

There is absolutely no difference between the Deldare made in 1908 and 1909 and that made after World War I (1923, 1924, 1925), except the date. Both issues of Deldare were made of semivitreous china, from the same formula, and were hand-decorated by the same method. In fact, some of the same artists worked on both the late and early ware. Some collectors have found later pieces that they consider inferior to the early ones, and so believe that all later Deldare is inferior or made in a different manner. This is a fallacy. There is excellent work in both series. When early and later pieces showing identical scenes are compared side by side, no appreciable difference can be detected. Of course, one must take into consideration the abilities of the individual decorators—some pieces in both early and late Deldare are superior to others of the same period.

Virtually every piece of Deldare made in the years mentioned bears on the bottom its date of manufacture as well as the words "Made at Ye Buffalo Pottery—Deldare Ware Underglaze" (Ill. 20). A few pieces are found undated or with the date practically illegible. This fault cannot be construed as detrimental to the piece; rather, it merely indicates carelessness or an oversight on the part of the employee responsible for applying the trademark. Conversely, some pieces of Deldare are marked with two dates. For this, again, there is no explanation except carelessness, unless perhaps a piece was made in one year and distributed in another, and a second date added to indicate the year of distribution. Emerald Deldare has its own distinguishing mark on the bottom: "Buffalo Pottery Emerald Deldare Ware Underglaze" (Ill. 20) and the year 1911.

The discontinuance of Deldare Ware in 1911 and 1925 cannot be blamed on a lack of artistic acceptance, but only on the extremely high cost of manufacture. This can be readily understood. Each piece of Deldare was painstakingly hand-decorated on top of the transfer print (Ill. 114), and the highest quality of work was expected from each decorator. At the peak of Deldare production there was a decorating force of not more than fifteen men and women; generally, the force was smaller. A decorator could finish approximately two dozen dinner plates in an eight-hour working day, a small output per worker.

If the decoration and quality of the wares were not up to the expected standard, the pieces were classified as seconds, thirds, and even fourths, and sold at a greatly reduced price. This practice naturally added to the price that had to be put on the ware that was perfect in every way. Thus, when first-quality ware reached the store, it was priced out of the reach of the average budget.

Deldare was sold at many leading stores throughout the country. Although complete dinner sets were available, it was a widespread practice to buy only a few pieces at a time because of the high price. A small teapot, for example, sold for $10.00 in a department store—at a time when that sum represented considerably greater purchasing power than it does now. Deldare Ware was regarded with so much respect that it was often given as a special gift when something particularly fine was called for. In addition to dinner sets, Deldare was made in tea sets that came with an extremely attractive rectangular tray and a round tea tile. There were also a dresser set with tray, and vases, drinking sets, pitchers of various sizes, chocolate sets, and numerous other pieces.

The assumption is that Deldare was conceived as a probable Larkin premium. However, this objective was not realized at the beginning. Not until the Larkin fall/winter catalog of 1922–1923 was Deldare offered as a premium—for the first and only time. Since the response was not as enthusiastic as had been expected, it was not listed again. The lukewarm public reception of the Deldare premium may possibly be blamed on the pictorial deficiencies of the catalog presentation, which was entirely in black and white, though the color of the ware was clearly described in the text. (See Ill. 115 for the catalog page offering Deldare.)

To a very limited extent, Deldare was used in hotels and restaurants (Ill. 236), but the pieces were not embellished with the usual English-type decoration. The design or monogram chosen by the particular firm was used as decoration instead.

DELDARE DECORATIONS

The distinctive appeal of Deldare Ware stems for the most part from the unusual color combinations of the vivid decorative scenes against the delicate olive-green body tone. However, the brilliant, lucid overglaze adds much to the beauty of the ware. This apparently nondeteriorating glaze has preserved the Deldare scenes in prime condition on most pieces.

The year 1908 saw the introduction of the Fallowfield Hunt scenes on Deldare, which were reproduced from the colored scenes drawn by the renowned English artist Cecil Charles Windsor Aldin, who was born in 1870 and died in 1935. (Two of these are shown in Ills. 117 and 119). The Fallowfield Hunt series portrayed the sequence of an English fox hunt, with the following titles: "Breakfast at the Three Pigeons," "The Start," "The Dash," "Breaking Cover," "The Fallowfield Hunt," "The Death," "The Return," "The Hunt Supper," and "At the Three Pigeons." The scenes and colors of the original prints were faithfully executed on Deldare. The Fallowfield Hunt was done only on Deldare dated 1908 and 1909. Postwar pieces have never been found with this decor.

According to information supplied by the British Museum, the Fallowfield Hunt scenes done by Cecil Aldin were not made originally as illustrations for a book. Apparently the prints were published individually as decorative items and sold for framing—they are frequently to be found on the walls of country houses and inns. The authors have personally seen four framed Aldin prints, each one bearing his uniquely written signature, along with the date 1900 and "copyrighted by Richard Wyman and Co. Limited, 16 Bedford St., Strand, London, W.C.—Goffart Printers, Brussels."

Scenes of English village life in "Ye Olden Days" (Ills. 138–169) were also introduced as a Deldare decoration in 1908. They were used on 1909 wares as well and the postwar (1923, 1924, 1925) pieces of Deldare. All aspects and features of village life were depicted—"Ye Village Gossips," "Street Scenes," "Dancing Ye Minuet," "Ye Town Crier," "Ye Village Tavern," "Ye Lion Inn," "Ye Village Parson," "Ye Village Schoolmaster," "Ye Olden Days," "Traveling in Ye Olden Days," and many others. The source of many of the English scenes is not known. Some came from books such as Goldsmith's *The Vicar of Wakefield* and Mrs. Gaskell's *Cranford*. For example, a 6-inch tea tile titled "Traveling in Ye Olden Days" (Ill. 140) bears the same scene as appears in a *Cranford* illustration drawn by Hugh Thomson. In the book the scene is titled "Implored the Chairman."

Many of the phrases that appear on Deldare scenes—"To Spare an Old Broken Soldier," "His Manner of Telling Stories," "To Advise Me in a Whisper," "All you have to do to teach the Dutchman English," and others—can be found in *The Vicar of Wakefield*. However, none of these was found illustrated by a drawing in any of the many editions of *The Vicar* the authors examined at numerous libraries and museums. It is possible that these scenes are original illustrations by Buffalo Pottery artists, but evidence to substantiate that possibility remains elusive.

"Ye Lion Inn," a series of English tavern scenes (Ills. 170–178), was depicted on Deldare in each of the various years that Deldare was produced, both the early and late issues.

Much of the Emerald Deldare (Ills. 179–222) was decorated with Dr. Syntax scenes. The humorous verses about Dr. Syntax and the vivid illustrations date from early in the nineteenth century when (between 1812 and 1821) they were issued as *Tour of Dr. Syntax in Search of the Picturesque, Tour of Dr. Syntax in Search of Consolation,* and *Tour of Dr. Syntax in Search of a Wife.* The original Dr. Syntax caricatures were painted in watercolors by Thomas Rowlandson; the verses that went with them were written by William Combe. Rowlandson is said to have sent one scene a month to Combe, who was in debtors' prison (he was often there), so that Combe could write appropriate doggerel to go with it; the two men did not meet during this time.

Dr. Syntax scenes were first reproduced on dishes very early—shortly after the Rowlandson drawings appeared in print—when Clews used them in a lustrous dark blue. The very first Dr. Syntax scenes reproduced on Buffalo wares were also done in blue (Ills. 362 and 363). Dated 1909, these dishes have great similarity to the Staffordshire pieces.

In general, the Dr. Syntax scenes used on Emerald Deldare have been reproduced with a reasonable accuracy, though the artists who copied them from the original books for use at the pottery took some liberties—sometimes altering the minor details in a scene, often introducing oddities of punctuation and spelling into the verses, and also using some variations from the original coloring. To most collectors of Emerald Deldare, these evidences of the individuality of the artist are no detriment.

Incidentally, it is Deldare with Art Nouveau borders that is called Emerald Deldare. Though the various borders of this kind are similar to one another, they are by no means exactly alike. The border motifs on Emerald Deldare are sometimes entirely geometric (Ill. 202). At other times geometrics are combined with natural objects such as flowers, leaves, and butterflies, and various flowing lines and forms (Ill. 185). Emerald Deldare pieces not bearing a Dr. Syntax scene may be totally Art Nouveau in character—the central design as well as the border (Ill. 197). And in many instances a piece had all-over Art Nouveau decoration (Ill. 194).

It is not known for certain how the name Emerald Deldare came to be chosen to identify this ware, but the predominance of green in the decoration no doubt was an influential factor. Emerald Deldare has its own distinguishing trademark on each piece, along with the date, which was nearly always 1911 (Ill. 20). For some unexplained reason, there are a very few rare pieces with a different date. One such piece, a jardiniere dated 1910, is shown in Ill. 187. Besides the short period of manufacture, another reason for the scarcity of Emerald Deldare is that even fewer pieces were produced than might have been expected in that length of time because the decorations were more time-consuming to do than the conventional Deldare decorations. Nonetheless, today's avid collector can—with patience—find a piece or two of Emerald Deldare to add to his collection.

DELDARE DECORATORS

Although formally trained artists such as Ralph Stuart and Robert Helmich both supervised others and painted Deldare themselves, most of the decorators had no formal training. Helmich, a German ceramic artist, designer, engraver, and printer, was always spoken of with much respect by fellow workmen, who greatly admired his varied talents. He had served an apprenticeship in Germany, later worked in English potteries, and then at Shenango Pottery in New Castle, Pennsylvania, before coming to Buffalo Pottery, where apprentices with artistic ability were taught to work on Deldare. Buffalo Pottery apprentices were paid very low wages; when they graduated to journeymen, they worked on a piece-work basis. In 1908 and 1909, a top-notch ceramic artist paid on that basis could attain the magnificent salary of about $12.00 a week.

When the decorators reported for work in the morning, each one was given a stack of biscuit Deldare to be decorated (Ill. 114). The number of pieces decorated in a day depended on the artist's speed and ability, the size of the pieces, and the intricacy of the design. A decorator worked on several pieces at one time, doing the darkest colors first and the lightest ones last. There was, however, no wait between the application of the various colors, and it took considerable skill on the part of the decorators to keep the paints from running together. Deldare artists had the responsibility of mixing their own colors; this they did by blending a powder base of color with turpentine or fat oil.* When the color applications were completed, the pieces were stacked on stilts to avoid smearing the paint; then they were fired in a kiln to set the colors. After the firing, they were taken from the kiln for glazing, then refired.

Each color was put on a Deldare piece according to a rigidly prescribed pattern. The only latitude the decorator had was in painting the white clouds—these he could put in at his discretion.

The artist's name or initials can be found on practically every piece of Deldare. The earlier pieces were usually marked with initials only, but as the work force grew and there was more than one employee with the same initials, the decorators were required to sign their names. Curiously this signing had nothing to do with having a sense of pride in one's work. Rather, it pointed out the identity of any artist whose work was not up to the usual high standards. Many of the signatures are legible and can be easily read; others are practically illegible, extremely hard to decipher because of the decorators' idiosyncrasies in applying them. Some of the earliest decorators of Deldare—M. Gerhardt, Lita Palmer, Anna Delaney (Mrs. Ralph Stuart), Helen Biddle, and Kathleen Caird—graciously provided the authors with considerable information about this ware.

Below is a list of the initials and signatures that have been found on Deldare Ware:

A. B.	G. B.	L. B.
A. W.	G. H. K.	L. P.
B. S.	G. H. S.	M. G.
B. W.	G. M.	M. H. F.
C. A.	G. O.	R. S.
C. B.	G. R.	R. W.
C. D.	H. B.	T. N.
D. W.	H. M. B.	W. E.
E. B.	K. E. K.	W. F.
	K. E. S.	

---

* Turpentine that has been allowed to evaporate partially, so that it becomes thicker. Colors mixed with it before application will not run together.

L. ANNA	A. JENTSHI	M. SIMPSON
H. BALL	G. H. JONE	R. SIMPSON
G. BEATTY	KATON	W. E. SIMPSON
L. BERKS	J. KEKOLA	M. SNED or M. SNEDEKER
H. BIDDLE	A. LANG	O. SOUTER
M. BIDDLE	F. MAC	M. STEINER
E. BROEL	ED J. MARS	STILLER
M. BROEL	E. MISSEL	L. STREISSEL
M. BRON	L. MUNSON	R. STUART
K. CAIRD	J. NAKOLK	TARDY
E. DITMARS	L. NEWMAN	M. THOMPSON
E. DOWMAN	L. PALMER	A. WADE
FARDY	M. RAMLIN	WAYSON
H. FORD	W. RAMLUS	WHITFORD
W. FOSTER	G. REATH	J. WIGLEY
J. GERHARDT	H. ROBIN	L. WIL
M. GERHARDT	A. ROTH	M. J. WILSON
P. HALL	F. ROWLEY	B. WILTON
HARRIS	E. SAUTER	R. WINDSOR
M. HLUMNE	O. SHAFER	L. WIT
P. HOLLAND	N. SHEEHAN	R. VAISE
HONES		N. VOGT

This is not a complete listing of decorators, nor is it certain that there is not some duplication of names and initials. For example, "H. B." may be the same person as "H. Ball," or "E. B." and "E. Broel" may be one person.

Any piece of Deldare decorated in other than Old English scenes is commonly known as a Deldare Special (Ills. 223 and 227). Such pieces have the Deldare body, but vary widely in subject matter, design, and form. For the most part, they are rarer than regular Deldare. In many cases, they are not even marked with the usual Deldare mark, but most are dated and carry "Buffalo Pottery" on the bottom. The dates also differ to some extent from the dates on regular Deldare. Dates of 1907, 1910, 1914 are to be found on some of the items.

No records remain to tell why these pieces were produced, but our studies lead us to believe that they were made by special request. Many people who own a Deldare Special piece believe that theirs is one of a kind, though we have seen duplicates of most such items. Some, no doubt, *were* one of a kind in decor— done as an experiment or to satisfy the whim of an executive or an important customer. Also, it was by no means uncommon for an artist to design and decorate a piece of Deldare or any other Buffalo pottery with an original pattern of his own creation, in his spare time perhaps.

All the special items known to the authors are pictured in this book, but doubtless many more exist and will come to light in the future. Among the known specials are the Days of the Week plates (Ills. 224 and 225), the Lost plate (Ill. 220), Indian Scenes mug (Ill. 231), and the Sailor Humidor (Ill. 227). So few of these special creations have been found and so great is the demand for them that they are priced as high as the finest of antiques today.

Although many people believe it is only in recent years that Buffalo pottery and Deldare in particular have reached such a peak of recognition, this idea is entirely erroneous. The excerpts that follow are taken from articles written in 1910 and 1913 respectively, only two of many articles that could be cited to illustrate the esteem in which the firm and its wares were held in its own day.

The first excerpt is taken from "Live Wire," published by the *Journal of Commerce, Niagara Area:*

DELDARE ART WARE

Comparatively few Buffalonians know that pottery is manufactured on a large scale in this city. It is quite probable that there are more people outside of Buffalo who know of and value the products of this particular industry than within the city limits. Besides manufacturing the ordinary lines of pottery, suitable for home and hotel use, it has gained distinction by several of its art and decorative lines.

This concern—the Buffalo Pottery—was the first to manufacture, in America, Blue Willow Ware. . . . Another class of decorated ware is that which illustrates the three tours of Dr. Syntax . . . created and made famous by Rowlandson, the famous English caricaturist. The . . . Buffalo concern is now manufacturing a large number of these pieces, and some of the best critics say they are equal to the originals [obviously, the Clews Dr. Syntax plates].

The Buffalo Pottery is entitled to still greater distinction through the manufacture of what is called its "Deldare Ware." This is considered by those who know to be a distinct addition to American ceramics. It is an entirely original production, so artistic in every detail that it has attracted the favorable attention of leading pottery experts. Moreover, a Buffalonian, traveling in Great Britain a few months ago, accidentally discovered that one of the leading potteries of that country was attempting to copy "Deldare Ware." When the English superintendent was questioned about it, he said that, so far as he knew, it was the first case on record where an English or French potter had ever attempted to copy any American design or particular kind of ware. This fact is of great significance and one in which every Buffalonian can take a natural pride.

Among the series of decorations is the famous "Fallowfield Hunt." Four scenes are used: "The Hunt Breakfast at the Three Pigeons," "The Hunt," "The Death," "The Dinner After the Hunt." The decorations are Old English in effect, all the costumes, attitudes and characters being those of from 1700 to 1800. Many of the Old English books have been searched for ideas and quaint illustrations. Some of these are illustrative of famous English classics, such as *The Vicar of Wakefield,* "Miss Mattie in the Sedan Chair," in *Cranford,* and other subjects. The *Brooklyn Eagle* said editorially: "The picturesque interiors of 'Ye Olde Lion Inn,' 'Ye Village Tavern' and so on are made decorative centers for some of the pieces. It is hard to realize their unusual attractiveness without seeing them."

A new line of Deldare is now being worked up for next year. Its illustrative features will include the Dr. Syntax tours in underglazed colors—greens, browns, yellows and whites.

The second article, written by Marion Harland, was titled "My Trip Through the Larkin Factory." It was published by the Larkin Company in 1913.

About a mile east of the factories, Larkin Company owns and operates the Buffalo Pottery. It is modern and complete in every respect. Electricity is used here on a larger scale than in any other pottery in the country. The grounds cover seven acres.

I was told that the Company did not want to build a pottery, but was forced to erect and equip one, to prevent delays in delivery, and give its customers best quality by maintaining a fixed standard and protecting them from inferior workmanship.

Three hundred men and women are employed here. Beginning with domestic and imported clays, and ending with finished wares, everything is made under these roofs. The output includes a large variety of sets and pieces, for Buffalo Pottery Ware has an enviable reputation. There is a fine line of Tea, Dinner, and Toilet Ware, in underglaze and overglaze semi-vitreous porcelain. Results here obtained have not been surpassed by other American potteries.

The Deldare Ware made here is a valuable addition to the ceramic art, and appeals strongly to collectors and to those who want the best. Its body is olive green, of a peculiarly pleasing shade. It is easy to make a colored glaze on a white background, but this exceptional ware shows olive green throughout. That result is far more difficult to obtain. All the decorations are hand worked. As they are laid on in flat colors under the glaze, rich and attractive effects are obtained. I saw an array of quaint, artistic shapes in plates, tankards, pitchers, teapots, trays, steins, and bowls. Some of its unusual wares are bought by the most prominent firms in the country, but the Company operates the Pottery chiefly for customers' use. Here, in 1905, was made the first Blue Willow ware manufactured in America. Originals are daily reproduced with absolute fidelity, and the decorations are sharp and clear. Being under the glaze they are durable. Prior to 1905, all Blue Willow ware used in this country had to be imported from England. Those who own this porcelain should acquaint themselves with the interesting love-tale that gave rise to the pattern. It will be sent to all who ask for it. To know its motif makes the dainty service all the more interesting. I saw many beautiful examples of ware in gold and other attractive decorations; also the famous Dr. Syntax's designs, which first appeared in the old blue Staffordshire (England) china, now so rare. These designs are done here in Emerald Deldare, and for all practical purposes are good substitutes for originals, whose plates sell at Forty Dollars, and platters at Three Hundred Dollars. It is a significant fact that America's leading jewelry firm, for the first time in its history, recently bought a line of Buffalo Pottery ware for its china and porcelain departments. Before this, it had always refused to carry any American ware in stock.

Deldare ware is treasured not only for its beauty of color and interesting decoration but also for its high investment value. At the same time that it is adding to the charm of any room where it is displayed, it is also increasing in value at the rate of 30 to 50 percent a year. This trend has remained consistent for approximately six or seven years, with no sign of diminishing.

114. An old photograph, dated 1909, showing an employee hand-decorating Deldare Ware. *Courtesy of Harry H. Larkin, Jr.*

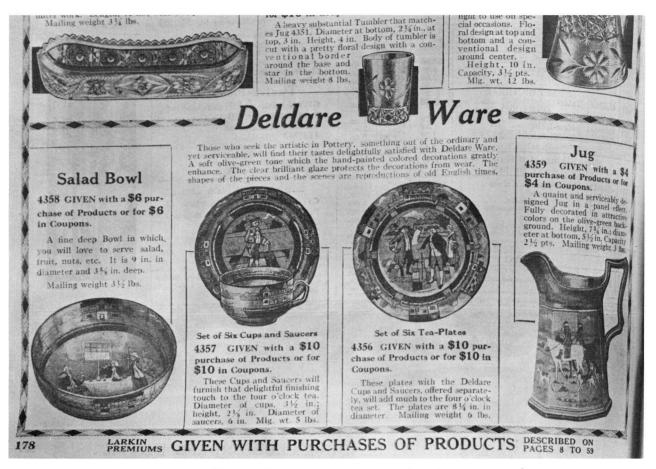

115.   Deldare was offered in the Larkin fall-winter catalog of 1922–1923. This was the only time Deldare was ever shown in any catalog. *Courtesy of Harry H. Larkin, Jr.*

116.   Salesman's sample Deldare plate, dated 1908.

117. A framed print (18 by 28 inches) of the Fallowfield Hunt scene, known as "The Hunt Supper," done in 1900 by the English illustrator Cecil Aldin. This is only one of many Aldin scenes reproduced on Deldare. Note Aldin's unique signature in the lower-right corner. *Courtesy of Dr. and Mrs. John W. Prout.*

118. In the center is a 12½-inch tankard-type pitcher decorated with the same scene shown in Ill. 117. Most of the details of Aldin's Fallowfield Hunt scenes were carefully reproduced on Deldare. The tankard is signed "M. Caird." The two mugs, both 4½ inches tall and dated 1909, bear the title "The Fallowfield Hunt." They are signed, respectively, by M. Gerhardt and J. Gerhardt, who were sisters. M. Gerhardt is still alive.

THE FALLOWFIELD HUNT.
THE BREAKFAST AT THE THREE PIGEONS.

119. Another Cecil Aldin print, same size and date as the print in Ill. 117. This one is called "The Breakfast at the Three Pigeons." Again, note Aldin's signature. *Courtesy of Dr. and Mrs. John W. Prout.*

THE FALLOWFIELD HUNT
BREAKFAST AT THE THREE PIGEONS

120. A 12-inch wall plaque decorated with a copy of the scene shown in Ill. 119 and labeled "The Fallowfield Hunt—Breakfast at the Three Pigeons." The plaque is dated 1908 and signed "N. Sheehan."

121. Dated 1908, this 14-inch chop plate is labeled "The Fallowfield Hunt, the Start," and signed (on the front) "J. Gerhardt."

122. Group of Fallowfield Hunt Deldare mugs. The three larger ones (from left to right) are described as follows: 3½ inches tall, 1909, "Breaking Cover," signed by R. Caird; 4½ inches tall, 1908, "At the Three Pigeons," signed by E. Ditmars; 3½ inches tall, 1909, "Breaking Cover," signed by B. Wilton. The two small mugs both measure 2½ inches. The one at left, titled "The Fallowfield Hunt" and dated 1909, is signed by F. Mac. The one at right, dated 1924 and unsigned, is called "Scenes of Village Life in Ye Olden Days."

123. Signed by L. Streissel and dated 1909, this 8½-inch Deldare plate is titled "The Fallowfield Hunt, The Death."

124. Deldare plate, 10 inches in diameter, is titled "The Fallowfield Hunt, Breaking Cover." It is dated 1909 and signed by H. Biddle.

125. Nine-inch Deldare bowl titled "The Fallowfield Hunt, the Death" is dated 1909 and signed by W. Foster. Bowl is 3¾ inches deep.

126. Octagon-shaped, 8-inch Deldare pitcher is dated 1909 and signed by P. Hall. Title (near the bottom) reads: The Fallowfield Hunt, The Return.

129.   Deldare calling-card tray 7¾ inches in diameter, dated 1908 and titled "The Fallowfield Hunt." Tray is signed by O. Sauter. *Courtesy of the Buffalo and Erie County Historical Society.*

127.   This 10-inch pitcher is shaped similarly to the one in Ill. 126 and bears the same date, but the signature is illegible. Title (near the bottom) reads: "The Fallowfield Hunt, Breaking Cover."

128.   Deldare cups and a saucer, 1909, titled "The Fallowfield Hunt." Signed by Ed. J. Mars. (Second cup is same as first but turned to show opposite side.) *Courtesy of Buffalo and Erie County Historical Society.*

130. Nine-inch Deldare soup plate dated 1909 and signed by E. Dowman. The title is "The Fallowfield Hunt, Breaking Cover."

131. Titled simply "Breaking Cover," this 5-inch sauce dish is dated 1909 and signed by R. Windsor. *Courtesy of the Buffalo and Erie County Historical Society.*

132. M. Bron signed this 6½-inch Deldare plate titled "The Fallowfield Hunt." Date is 1909. *Courtesy of the Buffalo and Erie County Historical Society.*

133. Signed only with the initials "M.H.F.," this 9¼-inch Deldare plate is labeled "The Fallowfield Hunt, the Start." Date is 1908.

134. Unsigned Deldare six-sided open sugar, 1908, decorated with an uncaptioned Fallowfield Hunt scene. Width of bowl is 4 inches; height, 3½ inches.

135. Deldare relish dish, 1909, was signed by A. Lang. It measures 12 by 6½ inches, and is titled "The Fallowfield Hunt, the Dash." *Courtesy of Alice Herrmann Antiques.*

136. Unsigned Deldare bowl measuring 12 inches across, 5 inches deep, and dated 1909. Title is "The Fallowfield Hunt, Breakfast at the Three Pigeons." *Courtesy of Dr. and Mrs. John W. Prout.*

137. Deldare punch bowl profusely decorated with many of the Fallowfield Hunt scenes. It measures 14¾ inches in diameter and 9¼ inches in height, and is dated 1909. Signature is "W. Foster." *Courtesy of Mrs. Walter B. Robb.*

138. Deldare tea pieces, each one bearing the title "Scenes of Village Life in Ye Olden Days." The creamer, dated 1924, is signed "G.H.S." Small teapot, dated 1909, is 3¾ inches high, and is signed "C.D." Covered sugar, dated 1925, is signed "G.H.S." Here, early and late pieces bearing the same title can be compared.

94

139. Larger (5¾ inches) Deldare teapot than the one shown in Ill. 138, but bearing the same caption though decorated with different scenes. This one is dated 1924 and signed "G.H.S."

140. A 6-inch Deldare tea tile dated 1924, signed "T.H.," and titled "Traveling in Ye Olden Days." The scene is taken from an illustration by Hugh Thomson in *Cranford*.

141. Deldare tea tray, 12 by 10½ inches, is dated 1908. The decorator's signature ("W. Foster") can be seen at bottom left and the title of the scene ("Heirlooms") at bottom right.

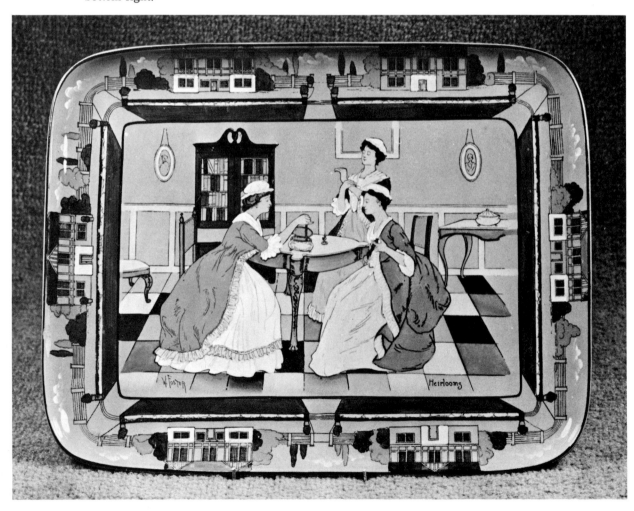

142. This 10-inch Deldare plate, dated 1908, bears the title "Ye Village Gossips" and the decorator's signature ("M. Snediker").

143. All three pieces of the Deldare dresser set, dated 1909, are decorated with village scenes. *Left:* Covered powder jar, signed by J. Gerhardt, is titled "Ye Village Street." *Center:* Pin tray, 6¼ by 3½ inches, is signed with the initials "E.B." and titled "Ye Olden Days." *Right:* Hair receiver, titled "Ye Village Street," is unsigned. (Another dresser set is shown in Ills. 237 and 238.)

144. A 1909 Deldare dresser tray, 9 by 12 inches, is titled "Dancing Ye Minuet" and is signed by M. Harrison.

145. R. Wade signed this 1908 Deldare plate. Title of scene is "Ye Olden Times. Diameter is 9½ inches.

146. An 8¼-inch Deldare plate dated 1908 and bearing a scene titled "Ye Town Crier." The initials "E.B." appear at the right.

147. Scene titled "Ye Village Street" decorates a 7¼-inch Deldare plate that is also dated 1908. Signature: "O. Sauter." *Courtesy of John A. Navagh.*

148. Ten-inch Deldare cake plate (1909) with "Ye Village Gossips." Signature (at right) is "E. Dowman." *Courtesy of Mr. and Mrs. Pat Cutini.*

149. "Ye Olden Times" scene decorates the 8½-by-6½-inch Deldare open vegetable server shown here. Date is 1909 and signature is "H. Ford." *Courtesy of Mr. and Mrs. Pat Cutini.*

150. Deldare teacup and saucer with title "Ye Olden Days" on saucer only. Date is 1909. Signature on saucer is "J. Nekolk"; on cup, "G. H. Jone."

151. "Ye Olden Times" Deldare relish tray measures 12 by 6½ inches. Date is 1908; signature (at right), "W. Foster." *Courtesy of Alice Herrmann Antiques.*

152. A 9-inch Deldare fruit bowl (depth is 3¾ inches) bears the title "Ye Village Tavern." It is dated 1908 and signed by H. Ford.

153. Deldare fern bowl measures 8 inches in diameter and is dated 1924. Title is "Ye Village Street," and signature, "G. Beatty." Originally, this bowl contained a ceramic insert to hold the plant. *Courtesy of Frank L. Withee.*

154. A 6½-inch cereal bowl in Deldare, dated 1908. Initials "H. B." appear at center right. Title is "Ye Olden Days." *Courtesy of Ada Jane Corbett.*

156. Deldare candlesticks, 9½ inches in height, dated 1909 and 1925 respectively. Both are untitled, but one at left is signed with initials "W.F." and one at right with "E.B." Some candlesticks (note the one at right) were made with a hole in the side or base for electric wiring, for conversion into lamps.

155. Deldare combination matchbox holder and ashtray is dated 1925 and signed with the initials "E.B." It measures 6½ inches long, 3¼ inches high. Title is "Scenes of Village Life in Ye Olden Days."

158. Front view of the shield-back candlestick shown in Ill. 157.

159. Combination candleholder and match holder 5½ inches in height. Scene is untitled, but this Deldare piece is dated 1909 and signed by B. Wilton. *Courtesy of Mr. and Mrs. Pat Cutini.*

157. Shield-back candlestick of Deldare, 7 inches tall, is dated 1909 and signed with the initials "G.R.", but does not bear a title. (See Ill. 158.) *Courtesy of Ada Jane Corbett.*

160. Untitled Deldare vase decorated with a village scene of by-gone days. Height is 9 inches; date, 1909.

161. Vase measuring 8½ inches is a dated (1909) but unsigned piece of Deldare. Scene facing viewer is titled "Ye Village Parson"; on reverse is "Ye Village Schoolmaster." *Courtesy of the Vogel family.*

162. An undated, untitled, 8-inch Deldare vase signed with the initials "B.S." On the reverse side is a highly fashionable man and woman. The authors have seen two other vases like this one, both also undated. *Courtesy of the Vogel family.*

163. Deldare chocolate set, with date 1909 and scene titled "Ye Village Street." Six-sided pot is 9 inches tall and is signed "Stiller." *Courtesy of the Buffalo and Erie County Historical Society.*

164. Tankard-type Deldare pitcher, 12½ inches in height, is dated 1908 and signed by M. Broel. Each side has a different scene, with titles taken from *The Vicar of Wakefield*. Facing the camera is "All you have to do to teach the Dutchman English"; on the other side is "The Great Controversy." The 3½-inch mugs, signed by E. Dowman, are identified as "Ye Lion Inn."

165. Six-inch Deldare pitcher, dated 1923, is signed with the initials "G.H.S." The title shown is "Their Manner of Telling Stories"; other side is titled "Which He Returned with a Curtsey" (both quoted from *The Vicar of Wakefield*).

166. Seven-inch octagon-sided Deldare pitcher dated 1923 and titled (one side) "To Spare an Old, Broken Soldier"; (other side) "To Advise Me in a Whisper." (Both are quoted from *The Vicar of Wakefield*.) *Courtesy of Mr. and Mrs. Pat Cutini.*

167.   Dated 1908 and signed "P. Hall," this 9-inch eight-sided Deldare pitcher bears (facing side) the title "With a cane Superior air" and (opposite side) "This Amazed Me" (both quoted from *The Vicar of Wakefield*). *Courtesy of the Buffalo and Erie County Historical Society.*

168.   Undated 8-inch Deldare pitcher with the title "To demand my annual Rent" on the side facing the camera, and "Welcome Me with most Cordial Hospitality" on the opposite side (both quoted from *The Vicar of Wakefield*).

169.   Deldare jardiniere 8 inches in diameter and 6 inches high is dated 1909. It was signed by P. Hall. Title is "Ye Village Street." *Courtesy of Mr. and Mrs. Ralph Stuart.*

170.   M. Sned signed this 14-inch Deldare chop plate dated 1909 and titled "An Evening at Ye Lion Inn." Holes drilled through the bottom rim make it possible to hang the plate.

171. Twelve-inch Deldare plaque dated 1909 has the title "Ye Lion Inn." Plaque bears the signature of P. Hall.

172. Deldare bread-and-butter plate (6¼ inches diameter) is dated 1924 and titled "At Ye Lion Inn." Signature is "E. Broel."

173. Deldare calling-card tray, also with the title "Ye Lion Inn." Date is 1909 and signature "L. Newman." *Courtesy of the Buffalo and Erie County Historical Society.*

174. Octagon-shaped Deldare humidor, 7 inches in height. Date is 1909; signature, "E.B."; title, "Ye Lion Inn."

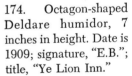

175. Unsigned Deldare nut bowl, dated 1909, titled "Ye Lion Inn." Diameter is 8 inches; depth is 3¼ inches.

176. "Ye Olde English Village" appears on the facing side of this 10-inch octagon-shaped Deldare pitcher dated 1909. Reverse side is titled simply "Ye Lion Inn." Signature is "H. Steiner." *Courtesy of Dr. and Mrs. John W. Prout.*

177. Deldare tankard, 6¾ inches high and dated 1924. Facing side is titled "Ye Lion Inn." Other side is "Ye Old English Village." This piece bears the initials "W.F." The white lining is an unusual characteristic that is found on few pieces of Deldare.

178. Identical 4¼-inch Deldare mugs placed so that both sides can be viewed. Date is 1908; title, "Ye Lion Inn." Signature is "M. Gerhardt." *Courtesy of Ada Jane Corbett.*

179. Emerald Deldare tea pieces, 1911. Covered sugar (unsigned), titled "Dr. Syntax in the wrong lodging house," reads "But with his day,s fatigue oppress,d / Syntax begged leave go to rest." (See the caption for Ill. 207.) Three-inch creamer, likewise unsigned, bears the title "Dr. Syntax with the dairymaid," / and reads: "Come here sweet girl don't be afraid / Tell me your cares he softly said." "Dr. Syntax disputing his bill with the landlady" is the title on the teapot, above the lines: "And for your beef— and beer and tea— / You kindly charged—me one pound three!" On the reverse side of the teapot appears "Dr. Syntax copying the wit of the window." *Courtesy of Mr. and Mrs. Pat Cutini.*

180. Emerald Deldare tea tray (1911) measures 13¾ by 10¼ inches. Signature is "R. Stuart." The title of the scene is "Dr. Syntax mistakes a gentleman's house for an inn." The verse reads: "Thus Syntax ate and drank his fill, / Regardless of tomorrow's bill, / He rang the bell and called the waiters, / To rid him of his shoes and gaiters." *Courtesy of Mr. and Mrs. Pat Cutini.*

181. Two identical Emerald Deldare cups and a saucer, signed by M. Ramlin. Cup is titled "Dr. Syntax at Liverpool," and reads: "And soon a person we address'd, / Whose paunch projected from his breasts." Cup is signed with the initials "L.N." Saucer bears the title: "Doctor Syntax and the Bookseller." The verse reads: "My errand was to bid you look / With care and candour on this book: / And tell me whether you think fit / To buy, or print, or publish it." Signature is "M. Ramlin." *Courtesy of John A. Navagh.*

182. Six-inch Emerald Deldare tea tile, 1911. The title is "Doctor Syntax / Taking possession of his living." The lines read: "At length, dear wife," he said, "we're come / To our appointed, tranquil home." H. Robin signed this tile. *Courtesy of Dr. and Mrs. John W. Prout.*

183. Octagon-shaped Emerald Deldare fruit bowl and matching tray 14 inches long. Bowl is 6¾ inches high and 10 inches in diameter. Decoration is completely Art Nouveau, a combination of floral and geometric motifs. *Courtesy of the Vogel family.*

184. "Dr. Syntax reading his tour" is the title on this Emerald Deldare 9-inch fruit bowl. (Depth is 3¾ inches.) Signature is "M. Broel." The lines read: "Each hearer, as th' infection crept / O'er th numb'd sense, unconscious slept / The cobbler yawn'd, then sunk to rest / His chin reclining on his breast."

185. Two beautiful peacocks decorate the inside bottom of an Emerald Deldare fruit bowl (1911), which measures 5 inches deep and 12¼ inches in diameter. *Courtesy of June Salvatore.*

186.   Emerald Deldare fern dish, 3¼ inches deep, 8 inches across. The distinctive Art Nouveau decor highlights butterflies and flowers.

187.   Again on this 1910 Emerald Deldare jardiniere, butterflies and flowers are the chief motifs making up the Art Nouveau decoration. The jardiniere is 12 inches in diameter and 9 inches deep. *Courtesy of the Vogel family.*

188.   Eight-inch Emerald Deldare vase (1911). The decoration features the kingfisher, dragonflies, iris, and water lilies.

189.   Geometric and floral motifs are again combined in the Art Nouveau style of decoration on this Emerald Deldare vase, 1911. Height is 8 inches.

192. One of a pair of 9-inch Emerald Deldare candlesticks. The decoration includes a bayberry motif. Signature is "Sauter." *Courtesy of June Salvatore.*

190. "Dr. Syntax returned Home" is the title of 7-inch-high Emerald Deldare humidor (1911). Signature is "Wilton." The verse: "Yes, I've a mind, this whip to crack, / Upon your raw bon'd lazy back, / Yes puff away, but tis no joke, / For all my schemes to end in smoke." *Courtesy of Dr. and Mrs. John W. Prout.*

191. Reverse side of the humidor shown in Ill. 190.

194. These 3-inch salt and pepper shakers are among the very few Emerald Deldare items dated 1915. The all-over Art Noveau decoration combines geometric and floral motifs. Signature is "M.G." *Courtesy of Mr. and Mrs. Barry J. Rodgers.*

193. Emerald Deldare shieldback candlestick (hand grip on back of shield), 1911, is 6¾ inches tall. This piece is signed with the initials "M.G." The Art Noveau decoration emphasizes floral motifs.

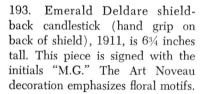

195. Combination matchbox holder and ashtray in Emerald Deldare (1911). Piece is signed by S. Rowley. The scene on the holder is one of trees against a lake and mountain background. *Courtesy of June Salvatore.*

196. Emerald Deldare inkwell set (1911), signed "A. Roth." The tray, 9 by 6½ inches, not only has the usual Art Noveau decoration, as do the inkwells, but also shows a scene in which two youngsters are playing with rabbits—a most unusual departure in the decoration of Emerald Deldare. *Courtesy of Mr. and Mrs. Pat Cutini.*

197. Toothpick holder, 2¼ inches high, not only has the Art Nouveau border of Emerald Deldare, but the body decoration as well is Art Noveau in feeling with the graceful flowing lines in flowers and leaves, and its geometric motifs. Signature is "M.G.B."

198. Twelve-inch Emerald Deldare tankard-shaped pitcher is signed "Newman." The lines under the scene read: To Becky's hand he gave a squeeze / And thus addressed her—"If you please / I'll taste your tempting toasted cheese." *Courtesy of Mr. and Mrs. Charles Spranger.*

199. Emerald Deldare tankard-shaped pitcher, 10½ inches tall. This rare white-lined piece dated 1911 is signed by W. Foster. The title is "Dr. Syntax Entertained at College." Below it are the lines: At, length the bell began to call / To dinner in the college hall / The provost, in collegiate pride / Plac'd Doctor Syntax by his side." *Courtesy of Mr. and Mrs. Barry J. Rodgers.*

202. A very small (2¼ inches) Emerald Deldare mug. Like the two preceding, this one is also 1911, but it bears the signature of A. Roth. The lines read: "I give the law to that are owing / The mean's that set these current's flowing / He loudly then pronounced the word / And straight the ruby bumper pour'd."

200. Mug (1911) bearing Dr. Syntax scene is 4¼ inches high. Signature is "L. Newman." The lines read: "Dr. Syntax again filled up his glass / A second toast proceeds to pass." *Courtesy of John A. Navagh.*

201. This Emerald Deldare mug is the same size and bears the same date as the one shown in Ill. 200. The title is "Doctor Syntax made free of the cellar."

203. Seven-inch Emerald Deldare card tray also bears the signature "A. Roth." The title is "Dr. Syntax robbed of his property." The lines read: "When soon as it was dawn of day / He gently seiz'd the fancied store / But as he passed the creaking door / Syntax awoke and saw the thief." *Courtesy of June Salvatore.*

C1. Deldare jardiniere and base (or garden seat), both dated 1909 and signed "Sheehan." The jardiniere (13 inches in diameter, 9 inches high) bears scene titled "Ye Lion Inn." The base (13½ inches tall) is decorated with two scenes, one titled "The Great Controversy," the other "All You Have to Do Is Teach the Dutchmen English." *Courtesy of John A. Navagh.*

C2. Punch bowl, dated 1909 and signed "W. Foster," is 9¼ inches high and 14¾ inches in diameter. It is decorated inside and out with various Fallowfield Hunt scenes. *Courtesy of Mrs. Walter B. Robb.*

C3. Two-piece Emerald Deldare fruit bowl is unsigned but is dated 1911. It is 6¾ inches high, 10 inches in diameter. The base is 14 inches long. *Courtesy of the Vogel family.*

C4. The largest known plate in Deldare is this Emerald Deldare plaque, which measures 16½ inches in diameter. The scene is titled "The Garden Trio." Plaque bears the usual 1911 date, and is signed "J. Wigley." *Courtesy of the Vogel family.*

C5. Deldare vase 22½ inches high, 11¼ inches in diameter, bears the signature of Stuart ("R. Stuart"), who hand-painted the decoration in beautiful colors. On the opposite side are cranes in their natural wild environment. *Courtesy of the Vogel family.*

C6. *Top row, left to right:* Gaudy Willow dinner plate; early hand-decorated plate in Bangor pattern; 1951 Christmas plate. *Bottom row:* game plate; geranium rose bowl; blue plate decorated with a Dr. Syntax scene.

C7. Service plates. *Top row, left to right:* plates made for the Majestic Hotel, the Chesapeake and Ohio Railroad, and Hotel Père Marquette; *bottom row:* for the Pacific Athletic Club and the Peter Stuyvesant Hotel.

C8. *Top row:* Mount Vernon plate (7½ inches); Gaudy Willow pitcher (8 inches); Niagara Falls plate (7½ inches). *Center row:* Pilgrim pitcher; Gloriana pitcher; Portland vase; cobalt blue vase with turquoise decoration and heavy gold encrustations and gold lining. *Bottom row:* pitcher decorated with Fallowfield Hunt scene on Blue Lune body; emerald-green vase with sterling overlay decoration; Elbert Hubbard medallion; Abino vase; Robin Hood pitcher with Deldare body.

204. The scene on this 8-inch octagon-shaped Emerald Deldare pitcher is titled "Dr. Syntax Bound to a Tree by Highwaymen." The lines read: "And fortune's angry frown bewailing, / A dog's approaching bark he hears; / Twas sweet as music to his ears; / And soon a sure relief appear's." *Courtesy of June Salvatore.*

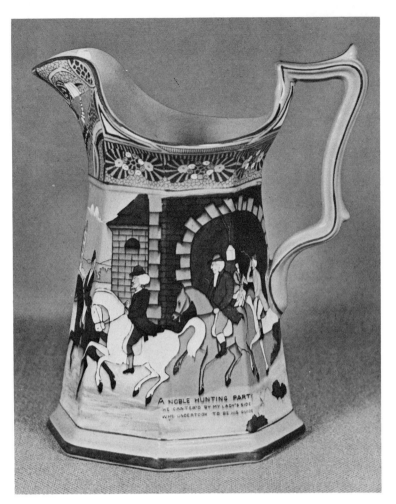

206. Also signed by R. Stuart is this 8¾-inch octagon-shaped Emerald Deldare pitcher. The title is "Dr. Syntax Setting Out to the Lake,s." (Note the substitution of a comma for an apostrophe; obviously, neither one was needed. See caption for Ill. 207.) The verse: "Incurious Ralph, exact at four / Led Grizzle, saddled to the door. / And soon, with more than common state, / The doctor stood before the gate." *Courtesy of Mrs. Walter B. Robb.*

205. Ten-inch octagon-shaped pitcher, 1911, carries the signature "R. Stuart." The lines under the title "A Noble Hunting Party" read: "He canter'd by my lady's side / Who undertook to be his guide." *Courtesy of Mr. and Mrs. Ralph Stuart.*

207. On this 6-inch Emerald Deldare pitcher signed by H. Robin, the scene is titled "Dr. Syntax, stopt by highway men." The verse: "For now, with fierce impetous rush / Three ruffans issued from a bush / One, Grizzle stopp'd, and seiz'd the rein,s / While they all threat the doctors brains." (The misspellings "impetous" and "ruffans" are those of the pottery artists, since these words are correctly spelled even in early editions of *Dr. Syntax*. In the old days a printer might substitute a comma for an apostrophe if he lacked enough apostrophes, but the comma here [in "rein,s"] was the work of the Buffalo Pottery artist, and did not appear in the early *Syntax* editions. Oddly, in this case ["rein,s"], either mark would be erroneous; the correct word is simply "reins," as it appeared in the 1815 edition.)

208. Emerald Deldare plaque signed by J. Gerhardt, one of the finest decorators at the pottery, measures 12 inches in diameter. Under the title "Dr. Syntax, Sketching the Lake" the lines read: "Along the bank,s, he gravely pac'd / And all its various beauties trac'd / But Grizzle in her haste to pass / Lur'd by a tempting tuft of grass." *Courtesy of the Buffalo and Erie County Historical Society.*

209. J. Gerhardt was also the decorator of this 7¼-inch Emerald Deldare plate titled "Dr. Syntax Soliloquising." The couplet: "Quit, my sad sir, that odious chair, / With your grave melancholy air." *Courtesy of June Salvatore.*

210. Ten-inch Emerald Deldare plate (1911), signed by M. Broel. Title of the scene is "Doctor Syntax Making a Discovery." The lines read: "Thus, passing on, he chanc'd to see, / Beneath an overshadowing tree, / Patrick engag'd in am'rous guise / Devouring Susan with his eyes." *Courtesy of Mr. and Mrs. Pat Cutini.*

211. Emerald Deldare plaque titled "The Garden Trio" measures 16½ inches and is dated 1911. It is, as far as the authors know, the largest Emerald Deldare plaque ever made. Signature is "J. Wigley." The lines read: "Miss was too fast by many a bar, / The old-one was behind as far, / While Syntax strove their faults to cover / By smoth'ring one and then the other." *Courtesy of the Vogel family.*

212. On this 13½-inch Emerald Deldare chop plate the scene is "Dr. Syntax Sell's Grizzle." Plate is signed by A. Sauter. The couplet reads: "Where must we look her ears to find? / And faith, she's left her tail behind."

213 A. Emerald Deldare plate, 1911, is 9¼ inches in diameter. Signature is "M. Ramlin"; title "Syntax Star Gazing." The verse reads: "Noise which both the gazers drew / From their celestial interview / They saw by Patrick's luckless trips / The luncheon in complete eclipse."

213 B. Signed by E. Miessel and dated 1911, this 8½-inch Emerald Deldare plate bears a scene titled "Misfortune at Tulip Hall." The verse reads: "A shelf gave way, another follow'd, / Ma'am Tulip scream'd, The Gard'ner hallooed, / While Syntax join'd the gen'ral bawling, / And soon upon the ground was sprawling."

214. The center medallion, as well as the border on this 8¼-inch Emerald Deldare plate, is Art Noveau in character. Here again floral and geometric motifs are combined.

215.   Another of the Emerald Deldare plaques decorated and signed by M. Gerhardt. The one shown here, dated 1911, measures 12 inches. The elaborate decoration includes doves, a peacock in full splendor, and a garden setting. *Courtesy of Mr. and Mrs. Charles Spranger.*

216.   Although this 8¼-inch plate is dated 1909, and therefore was made before Emerald Deldare was in production, the decoration has an unmistakable similarity to that on Emerald Deldare. This piece does not have the usual Emerald Deldare trademark, which was used only on 1911 pieces. The signature of the decorator is "J. Gerhardt." Under the title "John Alden and Priscilla" appear the lines: "Onward the bridal procession now / Move to their new habitation." *Courtesy of Mrs. Walter B. Robb.*

217.   Emerald Deldare plaque, 13½ inches in diameter, dated 1911 and signed by R. Stuart. The scene is called "Penn's Treaty with the Indians." The lines below the title read: "We are met on the broad pathway of good faith / And good will, so that no advantage is to be taken / On either side, but all to be openness, brotherhood / And love." (Note how nearly identical are the borders on the plates in Ills. 216 to 219.) *Courtesy of Ada Jane Corbett.*

218. "Daughter of the Revolution" plate, 9½ inches in diameter, is dated 1909. Like the plate in Ill. 216, this one was made before Emerald Deldare was in production and so does not bear that trademark in spite of its Emerald Deldare characteristics. Signature is "B. Wilton." *Courtesy of Arthur C. Nenstiel.*

219. Ten-inch plate titled "Yankee Doodle" and signed by M. Broel is dated 1908—too early to bear the Emerald Deldare trademark in spite of its characteristic border. The Revolutionary scene appears to be an adaptation of Willard's famous "Spirit of '76." *Courtesy of John A. Navagh.*

220. Ralph Stuart signed this 13½-inch Emerald Deldare plaque (1911), and he also painted the original painting from which this scene was made. Title is "Lost." (Plates bearing this scene are signed either "R. Stuart" or "C. Harris.")

221. Emerald Deldare vase (1911) is 13½ inches in height. Between the typical borders is an outdoor scene with an upper frieze of butterflies and a lower one of flowering plants. M. Gerhardt, who signed this piece, said it was known as the "American Beauty vase."

222. Basket of Emerald Deldare, 13 inches overall, has the usual 1911 date and Art Nouveau decor featuring dragonflies, butterflies, and geometric motifs. *Courtesy of the Vogel family.*

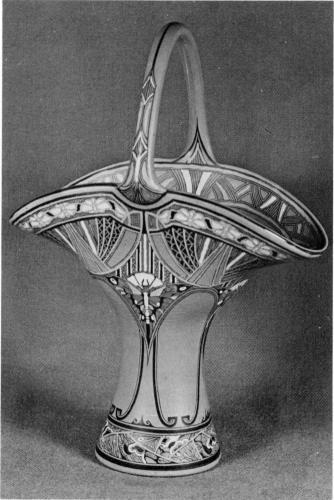

223. Deldare vase, dated 1914 and marked only "Buffalo Pottery," is 22½ inches in height. On the opposite side is shown a crane with a fish in its mouth. A vase similar to this one is dated 1917. Beautifully hand-painted in brilliant colors, both these striking vases were the work of Ralph Stuart and they bear his signature.

THURSDAY

224. Twelve-inch Deldare plaque dated 1914 and titled "Thursday" is of the two known that are decorated with a scene featuring friars. Signature is "J. Gerhardt." It is not known whether plates were made for the remaining days of the week.

FRIDAY

225. This twelve-inch plaque bears a scene giving the sequel to the one shown in Ill. 224: On "Friday" the friars are eating the fish they caught the day before. Here, again, the signature is "Gerhardt" but the initial is "M."

226. Undated, untitled Deldare plate picturing Spanish galleons is 8½ inches in diameter. Decoration is black except for the pink clouds. The back of the plate lacks the usual Deldare trademark and says merely "Buffalo Pottery."

228. L. Anna signed the 7-inch Deldare card tray shown here. It is dated 1908, and titled "Mr. Pickwick Addresses the Club." *Courtesy of Dr. and Mrs. John W. Prout.*

229. No title is given to the scenes that decorate this 12½-inch Deldare tankard-shaped pitcher, nor is there a decorator's signature. Bottom is marked only "Buffalo Pottery," without the usual Deldare trademark. *Courtesy of John A. Navagh.*

227. Deldare humidor, 8 inches in height. It is dated 1909, and signed with the initials "C. B." Lines on facing side read: "There was an old sailor, / And he had a wooden leg. / He had no tobacco, nor / Tobacco could he beg." The verse continues on the opposite side: "So save up your money, / And save up your rocks, / And you'll always have tobacco / In your own tobacco box."

230. Companion mugs to the Deldare tankard-shaped pitcher shown in Ill. 229 bear village and harbor scenes. They are 4½ inches tall and are dated 1907. *Courtesy of Harry H. Larkin, Jr.*

231. Deldare mug dated 1908 and picturing a bonneted Indian. It is 4¼ inches in height. The signature is "R. Stuart." Various other pieces of Deldare with Indian decoration have been found. *Courtesy of Dr. and Mrs. John W. Prout.*

232. Opposite side of the mug shown in Ill. 231.

233. Small (6¾ inches) untitled Deldare tankard dated 1911, with inner white casing. The English street scene is signed "R. Stuart." Note the elaborate gold decoration on the handle.

234. Deldare calendar plate for 1910 is extremely rare and in great demand. Diameter is 9½ inches; signature, "L. Anna."

235. The owl decoration on these 9-inch Deldare candlesticks is also a rarity. They are dated 1915.

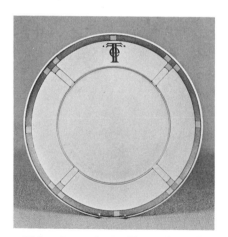

236. An early Deldare plate designed for a commercial account. It is undated and unsigned, and the TTE monogram has not been identified. The simple decoration resembles the Roycroft pattern, which also came in Deldare.

8

Abino Ware

POINT ABINO, A SANDY SPIT OF LAND JUTTING OUT INTO THE BLUE WATERS OF LAKE Erie on the Canadian north shore about fifteen leisurely miles from Buffalo, gave Abino Ware its name. The point itself inherited the name from a French Jesuit priest, Father Claude Aveneau, who lived there about 1690. Father Aveneau was one of the early missionaries who went into wilderness areas seeking to convert the Indians to Christianity. When the good father arrived at the point, only the Indians and a few venturesome Europeans had been there before him. Game abounded; wolves were common. Père Aveneau built himself a crude cabin on top of a hill, and there he communed with God to prepare himself for his years of effort among the Miami Indians at the mouth of the St. Joseph River in Indiana. He worked with the Miamis until 1707, when he was recalled. These Indians trusted and respected him, and they became so unruly after he left that Père Aveneau had to return to them. Eventually, worn out from his labors, the priest died in Quebec at the age of sixty-one.

First called Aveneau, then Abeneau, and now shortened to Abino, the point still has many of the same qualities that so impressed the French priest. It commands a magnificent view of the lake and the broad sandy beaches ringing the nearby bays. Its dunes, some of them seventy-five feet high, still are impressive, though hundreds of tons of sand were carried away years ago, for industrial purposes. Many of the original trees, some of them huge old black walnuts, were cut down to provide fuel for a lime kiln that once operated on the point. Yet the dunes remain, and new trees—tall poplars and pines—have replaced the old giants.

In season, Point Abino is a mecca for boating enthusiasts. Since the point juts out into the lake about a halfmile, it creates a natural bay that offers shelter from the violent southwesterly winds that frequently sweep Lake Erie. Even in the early days, sailing vessels found a haven behind the protective point in what is now Bay Beach, but the reefs off the point took their toll. The waters nearby hold the remains of many ships and barges. In the 1920's, a large lake freighter, heavily loaded with wheat and flax, ran aground on the reefs in a dense fog; its steel plates can be seen on the bottom on calm days. A U.S. Coast Guard lightship stationed about six miles off the point went down in a severe storm in 1913, with the loss of all twelve men who were aboard. Finally, in 1917, the Canadian government erected a lighthouse on the point, to warn ships of the danger.

The natural protected harbor that the bay affords attracted the Buffalo Canoe Club, founded in 1885 by William Lansing, and it moved its base from the waterfront of Buffalo to a site on the bay adjacent to the point, where it built a fine clubhouse. In the early days, the bay was frequently dotted with the tiny triangular sails of the sailing canoes the club members owned. Gradually these gave way to larger boats, some of cruising class, even to a considerable fleet of "R" boats. Because of the shallowness of the bay, these were replaced with twenty-one-foot Knockabouts of Canoe Club designs. Many Buffalo Canoe Club Lightning sailors have gained national and international fame, and club members have won many national and even world championships.

The Buffalo Yacht Club also built a clubhouse on the protected lee shore of Point Abino, in addition to its base in Buffalo. Like the Canoe Club, this organization remains very active today. Most summer weekends, when the westerly winds blow briskly, fleets of boats from these clubs, sails billowing in the breeze, can be seen riding the choppy waters of Lake Erie.

Sailing scenes reminiscent of an earlier day make up the distinctive decoration on most pieces of Abino Ware. In fact, this ware came into being in 1911, when the chief artist, Ralph Stuart, began to reproduce sailing scenes (Ill. 241) on a new line of items. Though the number and size of the sailboats pictured on the new wares varied according to the shape and size of the particular piece, the scenes clearly represented views of Point Abino and the surrounding waters, and so gave the ware its name.

Another decorative scene used on Abino Ware was also local in origin. This was the large, Dutch-type windmill that could be seen by anyone standing on the shore at Point Abino and looking eastward toward Buffalo. In 1832, the same year the city of Buffalo was incorporated, Silas Carter (he had served under Washington in the Revolution) built the mill on a site that later came to be called Windmill Point.

Carter, born in New Jersey in 1758, went to Canada after the war when England was trying to attract new settlers for her remaining American colony. He settled on "Windmill Point" in the early 1780's, and received a free grant of 400 acres from the government of Upper Canada. At that time Buffalo was nonexistent, there being little more than the log hut of an Indian trader on the site where the city stands now.

In those days it was no simple matter to convert wheat into flour. Unless the farmer took his grain to a mill, he had to grind it himself by one of two tedious methods. One was to use the slow, hand pepper mills supplied to the settlers by the government. The other, only slightly better, was to grind the kernels on the smooth top of a hardwood stump, using a flat stone roped to a springy sapling. Therefore, for many years Carter loaded his wheat, two bushels at a time, into a canoe and paddled down the lake shore and Niagara River to Chippewa Creek. There he would disembark, hoist the wheat to his shoulders, and follow the Indian trail to the mill at Niagara Falls. Late at night he would return with his precious flour, his load much lightened by the miller's fee.

After some particularly lean years, notably the "hungry summer" of 1816, also known as the "cold summer," and "eighteen hundred and froze to death," Carter decided to build a mill of his own. He felt himself better suited for the life of a miller than that of a farmer. There was plenty of limestone nearby, and he set up a kiln to burn the lime for the walls of the mill. One millstone was built up from broken boulders found on the farm, but the second run of burrstones was brought over on the ice from Buffalo. The three-story, sixty-foot-high mill was circular in shape, of the tower variety rather than the smock or post types also common at that period. A fantail projected from the cap, on the opposite side from the four sails, also called "sweeps" or "swifts." When the winds became too strong, the sails could be reefed, even furled, a necessary procedure during the strong gales that Windmill Point was noted for. Any gusty storm put a hard strain on the sweeps, and the miller had to be on guard constantly to unmesh the gears and furl the sails at a moment's notice. In fact, the miller's work never seemed to end. If the huge canvas-covered swifts did not need repairing, or if one or more of them had not fallen to the ground, then the inner machinery needed attention. The mill operated whenever there was wind, night or day; sometimes it would run around the clock to grind grain accumulated on windless days. In spite of the difficulties of operation, this mill was kept busy for more than forty years, some farmers coming as much as sixty miles to have their grist ground into flour. Such a trip would then take about five days, two days each way and one day at the mill. In the 1840's, farmers from Eden and other places on the American shore sometimes brought their grain across Lake Erie on the ice.

Indians long remained a source of danger to the mill customers. Farmers arriving in large grain canoes would stay well out from shore until ready to land close by—at a point just a few feet from the mill. Farmers coming by land quartered their stock in a small barn east of the mill, near Carter's house. The stone foundation of the house can still be seen.

The exact date the mill ceased operation is uncertain, but it is thought to have been at some time between 1875 and 1880. A few old residents can recall seeing the windmill operate in 1933. Today, abandoned completely, little more than a pile of weather-beaten stones, it stands a victim of the winds and rough weather that once provided its power. But Abino Ware pictures it in its heyday.

Although Abino Ware was generally decorated with seascapes, and sometimes the windmill on the point, the decorators apparently enjoyed a change of subject occasionally. A few pieces of Abino, mostly plaques, can be found with pastoral scenes. A rare plaque (Ill. 239), possibly one of a kind, bears a desert scene with the Pyramids in the background, and in the foreground a nomad astride his camel at an oasis. Other unusual pieces (Ills. 246 and 256) are titled "Portland, Me., Portland Head Light." These were probably commemorative or souvenir items, specially ordered through a jobber of Buffalo Pottery in the New England area. It was, as has been said earlier, common practice on the part of the firm to go to any lengths to accommodate clients and gratify their preferences.

For many years a rumor persisted that Abino Ware had originally been made for the exclusive use of the Buffalo Canoe Club. Research definitely proves this rumor to be without foundation. Abino Ware was intended to supersede Emerald Deldare as the prestige product of the pottery. It was produced in 1911, 1912, and 1913, the bulk of the ware being made in 1912. Whether, at that time, it was considered either a financial or an artistic failure is not known, but in any case production of the ware was discontinued. In all, it had been made for only a little over one year. Hence, Abino is scarce today, and quite understandably is priced nearly as high as Deldare Ware.

Only three artists worked on Abino Ware: Ralph Stuart, Charles Harris, and W. E. Simpson. Every piece is signed by one or the other of these three. Biographical details about Stuart appear in Chapter 2, but little information is available about the other two. It is known that Harris was of English origin, and because of his talent as an artist, was hired by the pottery to become Stuart's understudy. Questioned about Harris, surviving employees could remember little concerning him.

Abino Ware was made in exactly the same shapes as Deldare. In fact, Abino decoration was applied to the semivitreous Deldare blanks. However, Abino has unmistakable differences—its nautical themes and its colors. The main colors are rust and pale green. The scenes, instead of being boldly portrayed as on all other ware produced by the pottery, have a soft, subtle wispy appearance. They were done by means of transfer prints, then hand-decorated by the artists. An excellent overglaze has protected and preserved them.

The name Abino Ware is hand-printed in black letters on the bottom of each piece, along with the date of manufacture (Ill. 20). A group of three numbers also identifies each piece, the first number usually being a two. This numbering is used only on Abino Ware.

Abino was sold by jobbers of Buffalo Pottery to retail outlets throughout the country—china shops, gift shops, department stores, and so on. It was never offered in any Larkin catalog as a premium.

237. Abino hair receiver and powder jar have most unusual highlights of blue. They are dated 1913 and are signed by W. E. Simpson. *Courtesy of the Vogel family.*

238. Rectangular dresser tray hand-decorated with highlights of blue, unusual for Abino. Tray measures 10½ by 13¾ inches. Signature is "W. E. Simpson"; date is 1913. *Courtesy of the Vogel family.*

239. The desert scene on this 12-inch Abino plaque (1911) is a most unusual decoration to be found on Abino Ware. The original drawing was made by Ralph Stuart, and this rare piece bears his signature.

240. Abino plate dated 1912 and signed "C. Harris" is 10 inches in diameter. Practically all Abino bears a number that identifies the shape of the item. The number on the plate is 235. The windmill scene is a typical Abino decoration. *Courtesy of Arthur C. Nensteil.*

241. An *unnumbered* 12¼-inch Abino plaque dated 1911. This one is also signed "R. Stuart." *Courtesy of the Vogel family.*

242. Also unnumbered and dated 1911, Abino plaque is signed "C. Harris."

243. Abino bread-and-butter plates (6½ inches) are dated 1912 and signed "C. Harris." Both bear the number 231.

244. Abino plaque (13½ inches), dated 1912 and titled "In the Pastures." It bears no identifying number. The signature "R. Stuart" appears on the edge (at lower right).

245. Dated 1912, Abino plaque (13½ inches) is titled "The Waning Day." The scene was drawn by Stuart, and "R. Stuart" appears on the edge (at lower right). Plaque lacks an identifying number. *Courtesy of the Vogel family.*

246. C. Harris signed the 8½-inch Abino plate bearing the legend "Portland, Me. Portland Head Light," which was made for an unknown client, probably as a commemorative or souvenir piece. Plate is dated 1912 but carries no other number. *Courtesy of June Salvatore.*

247. Rectangular Abino tray (12 by 9¼ inches) is dated 1911 and signed "R. Stuart," but it has no shape number. *Courtesy of the Vogel family.*

248. Rectangular Abino tray (12 by 9 inches), dated 1912 and signed "C. Harris," bears the number 203. *Courtesy of Ada Jane Corbett.*

249. Abino sugar bowl (minus its cover) is also dated 1912 and signed by C. Harris. Identifying number is 297.

250. Abino teapot matches the sugar bowl in Ill. 249, not only in date and signature but also in its lack of cover. One distinctive difference is the presence of the letters "R Y" on the sail of the boat in the foreground. The authors have not seen such letters on any other piece of Abino. The identifying number is 251.

251. The shape number on the 9-inch Abino candlestick is 204. W. E. Simpson signed this 1913 piece.

252. Abino matchbox holder, 3¾ inches tall, with attached ashtray. This piece is dated 1912 and bears the number 224, but does not carry a decorator's signature.

253. Dated 1912, Abino basket signed "C. Harris" is marked with the number 215. Basket is 13 inches tall.

254. Seven-inch Abino tankard (1912) has a white inner casing. Signature is "C. Harris" and identifying number 264. *Courtesy of the Buffalo and Erie County Historical Society.*

255. Abino tankard-type pitcher is dated 1913 and signed by C. Harris. It measures 10½ inches in height and bears the number 249.

256. Seven-inch, octagon-shaped Abino pitcher bears the same date decoration and legend as the plate in Ill. 246. However, the pitcher is signed by "R. Stuart." Like the plate, it bears no identifying number.

257. Abino vase with typical seascape decoration bears the number 258. Eight-inch vase is dated 1912, and signed "C. Harris."

258. Small (6¾ inches) Abino vase with windmill scene and signature of C. Harris. Vase is dated 1912 and bears the number 261. *Courtesy of Mr. and Mrs. Ralph Stuart.*

259. C. Harris also signed this 6-inch Abino tea tile that is dated 1913. It carries the shape number 252. *Courtesy of Mr. and Mrs. Ralph Stuart.*

9

Christmas Plates

IN 1950, ROBERT E. GOULD, THEN PRESIDENT OF BUFFALO POTTERY, INTRODUCED THE firm's first Christmas plate. It was not made with the intention of selling it, but to be given as a Christmas gift to the employees, friends, and customers of Buffalo Pottery. The plate was so graciously received by all that first Christmas that presenting a Christmas plate became an annual custom.

Christmas plates were produced from 1950 through 1962, with the exception of 1961, a different design each year. The production of these plates served a dual purpose: they were used not only as Christmas gifts, but also served as experiments in color, body, and application of design. The designs were applied in various ways—by transfers, decals, and hand-applied colors. The 1957 plate was unusual because it came in five different combinations of body and design color. The 1962 plate was the only one that was edged in gold. Only 150 dozen of these approximately 9½-inch plates were made annually; the 1962 issue was limited to 75-dozen plates. Breakage and the elimination of seconds greatly reduced this number. The cost of producing each plate was estimated by the pottery to be four dollars.

The first two plates, 1950 and 1951, were designed by Eileen Travers, who was Mr. Gould's secretary. Mrs. Travers' artistic background made her well qualified for this task. Unfortunately, she did not sign her work. The following ten plates of the series were designed by a local artist, Rix Jennings, and his signature can be found on each of these except the 1962 issue.

The theme Jennings picked for the plates was taken from one of the most famous Christmas stories ever told, Charles Dickens's "A Christmas Carol." Generally, the scene pictured on the front of the plate was explained in detail on the reverse side. On some, however, the reverse merely extended "Season's Greetings." Along with each plate came a leaflet that also expressed Christmas greetings and told the story of the scene depicted.

The series actually ended with the 1960 plate, but at the special request of the Hample Equipment Company of Elmira, New York, a 1962 plate that was a composite of several previous Dickens scenes was designed for their exclusive use.

In initiating the Christmas plate series, President Gould hoped he was creating pieces that one day would be sought after by collectors. His dreams are being realized far sooner than he anticipated. Today, in antique shops throughout the country, the Christmas plates sell for $15.00 and up. The scarcest one is the 1962 plate. To purchase a complete set at one time is practically unheard of; however, Christmas plates do show up at auctions and antique shops from time to time, and with patience the collector can eventually complete a set.

135

260. The 1950 Christmas plate, solid blue in color.

261. The 1951 Christmas plate. Decoration and lettering are in green on a beige background.

262. Christmas plate for 1952, white with red decoration.

263. Varied colors are used on a white background on the 1953 Christmas plate.

264. The Christmas plate for 1954 is also done in a variety of colors against a white background.

265. Again in 1955, varied colors appear against a white background on the Christmas plate.

266. The 1956 Christmas plate, also in varied colors against a white background, the first one marked "Buffalo China, Inc."

267. Brown is used for the decoration on this 1957 Christmas plate, against a white center and beige border, but the plate was also made with other background colors.

268. The 1958 Christmas plate is ivory, with the decoration and lettering done in a variety of colors.

269. Pastel colors against a white background distinguish both the 1959 Christmas plate and the one for the following year.

270. The 1960 Christmas plate, with pastel-colored decoration against a white background.

271. The 1962 Christmas plate, the last one made, is white with green decoration and gold edging. (No plate was made in 1961.)

10

Commercial Service

UPON ENLARGING THEIR FACILITIES TO PRODUCE VITRIFIED CHINA IN 1917 (ILL. 9), Buffalo Pottery sought to widen its potential market with the manufacture of select institutional ware. The firm name subsequently became almost synonymous with individually designed dinnerware of the highest quality, their clientele including not only the largest hotels but also railroads, steamship companies, restaurants, commissaries, private clubs, hospitals, military and naval academies, government agencies, and many other institutions both public and private. The manufacture of such commercial ware continued for more than twenty years, to the late thirties. Then, with the country still beset by the severe economic depression, business fell off and the pottery gradually ceased production of customized institutional wares.

At the end of World War I, Buffalo Pottery was in an ideal position to cater to commercial and industrial accounts all over the world. Not only did it have adequate production facilities and an experienced and talented technical and art staff; it had a network of jobbing outlets that were already distributing the firm's products. Moreover, within the Larkin Company's vast complex there was already a division that catered solely to the wholesale distribution of equipment and supplies for hotels and restaurants—it was called the "Wholesale and Hotel Supply Division of the Larkin Company." Needless to say, when Larkin's totally owned subsidiary, Buffalo Pottery, started to produce artistic hotel ware, the parent company distributed this ware exclusively to their many established clients.

Jobbers would first get in touch with a possible account. If a spark of interest was shown, the pottery would create an individual crest, monogram, or design and submit it to the customer for his approval. Very often, the client was pleased and an order ensued. However, it was not uncommon for Buffalo Pottery artists to visit a prospective client's establishment first, before submitting a design, in order to make a more intelligent appraisal of his needs and tastes.

Probably the most beautiful pieces of dinnerware—without doubt among the most richly decorated ones—that the pottery produced were its service plates (Ills. 275 and 287). Perhaps they were made so because these largely decorative items need never be subject to food stains nor marred by fork and knife scratches. At any rate, Buffalo Pottery service plates were decorated with all the artistic skill of which the staff was capable. Most had either bands or intricate designs in pure coin gold, as well as vivid colors. On vitreous china, the decoration was usually applied under the glaze, but on these service plates the gold and some of the designs were put on over the glaze, since the gold would melt in the high temperatures needed to fire the glaze. After the gold was applied on top of the glaze, the pieces were fired in a kiln at a lower temperature. When they were removed, the gold decor appeared black. It had to be burnished to bring out its handsome luster.

Virtually every piece of institutional ware was marked "Buffalo China" (Ill. 19) on the reverse side. None, to the authors' knowledge, was marked "Buffalo Pottery." The earlier pieces (before 1930) occasionally also bore the name of the customer for whom they were made, as well as the date and the jobber. After 1930, in addition to these marks, the body color was specified too—Lune Ware, Ye Old Ivory, Rouge Ware, Colorido Ware, or Café au Lait. No artist's signature can be found on this ware.

Counted among the pottery's largest and most satisfied clients was the Chesapeake and Ohio Railroad. The creation of a china service for them, to celebrate the bicentennial of George Washington's birthday, called for the very finest expression of the chinamaker's art (Ill. 276). The objective was to create a service that had the grace of the colonial china that had adorned the hospitable tables of Washington's day and generation but that also possessed the qualities demanded by the modern way of life. The task was entrusted to Buffalo Pottery in 1932, and carried out with outstanding success. The crowning achievement in the creation of the set was the reproduction of the celebrated Gilbert Stuart "Athenaeum" portrait of Washington (Ill. 275), a true decorating triumph. To reproduce this portrait on the heavy rolled-edge ware ordinarily used in railway dining service was quite out of the question. It was necessary to re-create a dainty, thin service of old colonial shapes. Utilitarian considerations were subordinated to the effort to recapture something of the charm and the atmosphere that had prevailed in the dining room at Mount Vernon.

In making the George Washington set, Buffalo Pottery artists and artisans demonstrated they were still in possession of the techniques used to produce the tableware like that our forefathers cherished generations ago. No better evidence of their skill and care need be offered than the fact that to complete the service it was necessary to fire it four times under intense heat, twice before the reproduction of the Gilbert Stuart portrait of Washington.

The first, or bisque, firing was at 2400 degrees Fahrenheit and required seven days. The second, the gloss firing, was at 2150 degrees and required five days. Then the portrait was applied, and a third firing took place at 1500 degrees. Lastly, the gold was applied, and the set was fired the fourth and final time.

To reproduce Stuart's painting on china required what is known as the decalcomania photographic process. Nine different colors were used and fifteen printings were required to achieve the correct effect. The artists, working from a photograph of the celebrated painting, first made nine separate drawings on stone to catch the different shadings. Some appreciation of the required skill can be sensed from the fact that it was necessary to make these drawings backward.

Stuart's painting is distinguished by fine coloring and a lifelike expression. To reproduce it on china, preserving all the richness and beauty of the original, took literally many weeks and months of the lives of those who carried out the task. Each piece of the service passed through the hands of forty-seven persons during the course of its manufacture. The pure gold was applied by hand. On the service plates, it was applied by encrustation, which requires that the design first be eaten into the china with acid before the coin gold is applied. The effect can be produced by no other method.

According to Joseph Meidel, comptroller of Buffalo Pottery at the time, the gold on the George Washington service plate had a market value of about $5.00

per plate. The service plates were sold to the railroad for $66.00 per dozen, so it is obvious that the pottery took a loss on every plate sold. However, management considered the loss was offset by the prestige that accrued to the firm.

George Washington's association with the Chesapeake and Ohio Railroad is a fascinating historical sidelight. When, as a young surveyor, he explored the wilderness beyond the Alleghenies, Washington perceived the potential greatness of the western lands if they could be linked with the East. As he forded streams and climbed through mountain passes, he noted feasible routes for future canals and roads.

After the Revolution, Washington pressed his program for transport development. "Smooth the road and make easy the way," he wrote Governor Benjamin Harrison of Virginia, "and see what an influx of articles will be poured upon us; how amazingly our exports will be increased." As a result, Virginia chartered the James River Company to canalize that river westward from Richmond, and its shareowners elected Washington as company president. Thus, in 1785, four years before he was elected President of the United States, Washington became the head of the first commercial canal company in America.

Following the route that Washington himself had chosen, a 195-mile waterway was built and 200 miles of turnpikes connecting Richmond with the Ohio River. For many years the most important transportation artery in Virginia, by 1880 the canal was ready to give way to the railroads. The canal company became a railroad company, the Richmond and Alleghany, and rails were laid along the towpath.

Meanwhile, starting in 1836, the Chesapeake and Ohio Railway (originally called the Louisa Railroad, and later the Virginia Central) had also pressed westward from Richmond. Its tracks, lying north of the canal, reached to the headwaters of the James and, by 1873, along Washington's route over the Alleghenies to the Ohio River. In 1890, the Richmond and Alleghany, heir to the canal, was acquired by the Chesapeake and Ohio. Thus was fulfilled, to a degree he could not have foreseen, George Washington's dream of "making easy the way" between East and West.

Because the traveling public was so enthusiastic in its approval of the "Washington Ware" and so eager to own pieces of it, a limited number of service plates and other items, suitably packed, were available for purchase on the crack train, the George Washington. These were sold without profit by the railroad; the steward carried a price list for anyone interested (Ill. 277), and many a traveler gladly bought one or more items as souvenirs of the journey or to use as gifts. However, in the long run the Washington Ware proved too expensive for the railroad to maintain, and it was eventually retired from use and, through the years, sold to collectors. In 1952, the Chesapeake and Ohio Railroad donated a retired diner used on "The George," complete with a set of the George Washington service, to the National Museum of Transport in St. Louis, Missouri. This diner is now on public display at the museum.

In 1933, the services of Buffalo Pottery were again called upon by the Chesapeake and Ohio Railroad. This time, the order was to reproduce the Chessie Cat (Ill. 279), their corporate symbol, on china for use on the passenger train known as "The Sportsman."

Like a good many show-business personalities, Chessie was discovered by a public-relations man. It happened in 1933, when L. C. Probert, head of the Chesapeake and Ohio public-relations staff, noticed an appealing etching reproduced in the Sunday magazine section of the *New York Herald Tribune,* and had a flash of inspiration for capitalizing on the picture. The first step was obtaining the commercial rights to the etching, which was the work of Guido Gruenewald, a Viennese artist. Once this was done, the picture of the sleeping kitten was immediately put to use in a *Fortune* magazine advertisement (September, 1933) for the first all-air-conditioned train, the C&O's "George Washington." The picture was captioned "Sleep like a kitten on the Chesapeake and Ohio."

The response overwhelmed the Public Relations Department. Letters by the hundreds poured in requesting copies of the picture of the sleeping kitten, and in 1934, when Chessie became the C&O's calendar girl, the flood of letters reached fan-mail proportions. In the public's mind, the kitten Chessie had become the personification of the railroad.

After Chessie was adopted as the company's corporate symbol late in 1933, Chessie dinnerware was made for use on "The Sportsman." Eventually, it became the only pattern used on the C&O, but by then other American potteries were manufacturing the ware.

Another railroad that might be said to have figured in the story of Buffalo Pottery is the Baltimore & Ohio. This was the first railroad in the United States to be open for public traffic; its charter dates from 1827. The Enoch Wood firm of Burslem, England, made two blue-and-white plates commemorating the founding of the Baltimore & Ohio. These bore the name of the railroad on the reverse. On the front of one was pictured a typical *English* locomotive of about 1816— clearly, the English decorators had not seen an American locomotive and were unaware that the one they pictured was not used on any American railroad.

A number of firms vied for the opportunity of making blue-and-white dinnerware for the railroad's one hundredth anniversary. The plates shown in Ills. 282, 283, and 284 were among the pieces made by Buffalo Pottery in anticipation of being awarded the order. The borders of this ware consist of a sequence of pictures of railroad equipment—outstanding developments in the railroad's history and progress; but each type of dish has a different central scene. Buffalo Pottery did not, as it turned out, get the order; but today these pieces so carefully designed for a practical purpose have become highly collectible.

A unique order was given to the pottery by the Biltmore Hotel in New York City. In addition to the regular dinnerware (Ill. 301) that was made for the Biltmore, the hotel also ordered individually monogrammed handles of vitrified china into which silver table implements could be inserted. As far as the authors know, this item was not made for any other account (Ill. 354).

Mainly responsible for the decoration used on customized commercial services were Ralph Stuart, August Riehs, Perry Doncaster, and Frederick Krausen.

Stuart designed the earliest crests and custom-made plates until 1925, when he hired August Riehs (Ill. 274) to become his assistant. Born in Germany in 1892, Riehs served an apprenticeship in many of the famous potteries of Germany and Austria. As an apprentice ceramic decorator, he worked the first four years with no pay, and learned his trade well. Eventually he became a full-fledged journeyman and was employed as an artist by many of these same potteries. Hearing of the golden opportunities in the new world, Riehs and his wife, Anna, came to America in 1923. They settled in Rochester, New York, where he found immediate employment as a ceramic artist with the Smith Ceramic Studios. He remained there for two years. When he learned of a job opportunity at the Buffalo Pottery, he submitted samples of his artistic accomplishments for Stuart's approval. These made such an impression on Stuart that he wrote Riehs the job was his. Riehs remained with the pottery for thirty-three years, until serious illness forced him to retire. He died in 1967.

The authors have many of Riehs's original drawings; their intricacies and minute detail are amazing. Like Stuart, Riehs was an exceptionally good wildlife artist, and worked extensively on canvas as well as on china.

Krausen, both an engraver and artist during his long career, made many of the ornate borders found on commercial services. Krausen originally came to the pottery in 1921 at the age of sixteen. He decorated Deldare until it was discontinued in 1925; his signature can be found on many late pieces of Deldare as F F K, in letters that ran together. After his decorating job was abolished, he became an apprentice engraver under Perry Doncaster, who was then chief engraver, and following his apprenticeship he continued to work under Doncaster (except for a period of six years when he worked elsewhere) until 1945. In that year Doncaster left and Krausen became chief engraver; he is still with the firm at this writing. It is interesting to note that Fred Krausen thought so highly of Ralph Stuart's artistic capabilities that he at one time was enrolled as a student in Stuart's night art classes.

Exactly how many different designs (Ill. 272) were made for various institutions is not known, but research and the original patterns found lead one to believe that they numbered in the hundreds. That these wares received wide approval is attested by an article in the Buffalo *Courier Express* for July 6, 1930, written by George H. Wood, which mentioned the fact that Buffalo Pottery "vitreous-china hotel ware" was chosen by the U.S. Government as their standard of quality.

Since institutional ware made by Buffalo Pottery was used in almost every part of the United States and in many places outside this country, specimens of it should be readily obtainable in countless localities. As mentioned earlier, the collectible wares in this category were made largely between the end of the first World War and the beginning of the forties. Most are colorful and quite modestly priced; and since customized commercial services were made in endless variety, a novel collection of these wares should be possible at relatively small cost—unless the prices rise suddenly.

Undoubtedly, the George Washington plate is the highest-priced item of institutional ware. Long in the $50.00-plus category, it is certain to continue its climb into the $75.00 category and beyond in the not too distant future. Other commercial-service items scale down rapidly in price, depending on such varied factors as color appeal, the artistic merits of the specific decoration, one's interest in the organization or institution for which the ware was made, as well as the usual considerations of condition and availability.

At the end of the book is a quite comprehensive listing of scores of the commercial accounts for which Buffalo Pottery made customized tableware.

272.   Examples of the crests used to decorate commercial ware.

273. August Riehs, who designed the decoration for much of the fine commercial ware, painted this original watercolor. It was designed for use on a plate. *Courtesy of Mrs. August Riehs.*

274. Riehs designed this 9-inch plate for his personal use; it has his initials in the center. The decoration is in rust and green against a body of Ye Old Ivory. *Courtesy of Mrs. August Riehs.*

275. The 11-inch, gold-embossed service plate made for the Chesapeake and Ohio Railroad in 1932—for use on the "George Washington." These plates were probably the highest artistic achievement in commercial service of any pieces that the pottery ever made.

276.   Additional pieces of the Washington service. This ware was also sold to passengers. (See Ill. 277.)

The George Washington China Set

PRICE LIST

Ash Trays	$ .35	Plates		
Bakers		—Service	5.00	
—Large	1.20	—Dinner	1.00	
—Medium	1.00	—Breakfast	.80	
—Small	.60	—Salad	.65	
		—Bread and Butter	.55	
Bowls		—Soup	.95	
—Oatmeal	1.00			
		Platters		
Butter Chips	.55	—Extra Large	3.00	
		—Large	1.60	
Cake Covers	1.35	—Medium	1.20	
Celery Trays	2.20	—Small	1.10	
Creamers		Pots		
—Large	.65	—Hot Water	2.50	
—Small	.60	—Tea	2.50	
		—Stands	2.20	
Cups				
—After Dinner	.60	Saucers		
—Bouillon	1.00	—After Dinner	.35	
—Coffee	.75	—Coffee	.45	
—Courtesy	.35	—Courtesy	.20	
—Egg	.95			
—Mustard	1.00	Sauce Boats	1.25	
Fruit Dish	.45	Shirred Egg Dishes	1.00	

CHESAPEAKE AND OHIO LINES

Order Blank on Reverse Side

277.   A booklet distributed to its passengers by the Chesapeake and Ohio Railroad contained a price list for the George Washington China Set and an illustrated account of how and why the china was made, in addition to a timetable and menu (see Ill. 278). *Courtesy of Chesapeake and Ohio Railroad.*

278.   This picture of the inside of the dining car appeared on the menu mentioned in caption 277. Note the George Washington service plates on the tables. *Courtesy of the Chesapeake and Ohio Railroad.*

279. The "Chessie" cat service (1933) was also made for the Chesapeake and Ohio Railroad. It was designed for use on the train known as "The Sportsman." Shown here are a child's 7-inch feeding dish and a 10¾-inch dinner plate. The cat is gray; the lines, maroon. Body is Ye Old Ivory.

280. Check issued by the Chesapeake and Ohio Railroad as payment to Buffalo Pottery was reproduced on the bottom of an ashtray used on the "George Washington."

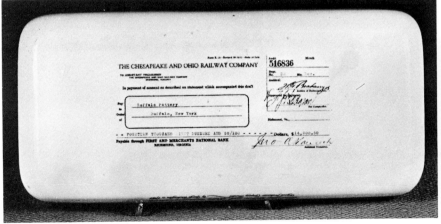

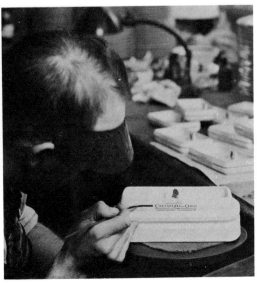

281. A picture taken at the pottery in 1932 shows an employee decorating an ashtray like the one in Ill. 280.

282. Dated 1927, the 9½-inch Baltimore and Ohio Railroad plate is titled "Harpers Ferry, W. Va." Decoration is in blue on a white body.

283. Seven-inch B&O plate titled "Thomas Viaduct, 1835." Date on bottom is 1927. Decoration is in blue.

284. A third B&O plate in blue and white. This one, also dated 1927, measures 8¼ inches and is titled "Potomac Valley." The historical border on this plate is exactly the same as on the plates in Ills. 282 and 283.

285. A plate from the service made for the Greenbrier Hotel has multicolor decoration against a white body.

286. Decoration in green on Ye Old Ivory body was chosen for the 1939 World's Fair service.

287. A 10½-inch service plate made for the Stuyvesant Hotel, Buffalo, New York, is rimmed with a wide band of green between two narrower bands of gold. Portrait of Stuyvesant is in brown tones.

288. The service made for the Roycroft Inn in East Aurora, New York, has green and rust decoration against an ivory background.

289. For Jack Dempsey's restaurant in New York City, his photograph was reproduced on Rouge Ware, under the glaze.

290. The service designed for the Chicago, Rock Island Railroad's "Rocket" was one made by the Lamelle process. Center is cream-colored; border, sage green, and lettering red.

291. A different pattern designed for the C.R.I. Railroad, but also made by the Lamelle process, with a sage green border.

292. Service plate made for the Barclay Hotel is decorated in gold and blue. Body is white.

293. The Montclair Hotel chose a white service decorated in red, with a gold edging.

294. Service plate for the Majestic Hotel has blue border trimmed with gold and a gold crest in the white center.

295. The 10¼-inch service plate, dated 1923, designed for the P.A.C. Decoration consisting of various bands and motifs is in gold, as is the crest centered against white. Narrow outer border is baby blue; inner border, yellow.

296. The crest on the 10¼-inch Hotel Cadillac service plate was done in a variety of colors. The wide band of maroon on the rim is bordered by bands of gold.

297. Decoration in maroon and black on Ye Old Ivory body make the 11-inch service plate of the Hotel Père Marquette an unusually striking one.

298. Dark blue decoration against a Blue Lune Ware body was made for the Fairview Golf Club.

299. A design in rust and black on an ivory body was made in 1927 for The Ahwahnee in Yosemite Park.

300. A service in the Old Abbey design was made for the Missouri, Kansas, Texas Railroad. The design is in brown on Ye Old Ivory Body; border is blue.

301. The Biltmore in Los Angeles chose a delicate design in gold and black on a white body.

302. In 1915, a peacock design was made for the Genesee Hotel. The background is white; the stripes are done in green and tan; the bird is in a variety of colors.

303. Service for the New York Central Railroad was decorated in brown on white, in the design known as Country Garden. This design was also made in other colors.

304. Around 1927, Pell's Restaurant chose a service with Ye Old Ivory body decorated with a multicolored fish and light green and black stripes.

305. A ski motif done in a green outline against a white body was one of the designs for commercial use.

306. A coaching scene with English overtones was reproduced in red on Ye Old Ivory body for the Fairview Grille.

307. Another design for commercial use, which was hand-decorated in a variety of colors on a Café au Lait body. The wide border was green.

308. A hand-decorated Rouge Ware plate made for a commercial account. The decoration is in blue and green.

311. Also for commercial use was this winter-scene design done in black and white on a Rouge Ware body.

309. A nautical design in blue on a white body that may have been made for a seafood restaurant.

312. Ralph Stuart designed a hand-decorated parrot on Ye Old Ivory body for a commercial account.

310. A commercial service with black decoration on a light-gray body.

313. White hot-toddy cups decorated with red devils were made for a commercial account. *Courtesy of Alice Herrmann Antiques.*

11

Miscellaneous Pieces

BUFFALO POTTERY MANUFACTURED A HOST OF PRODUCTS THAT HAVE NOT YET BEEN mentioned in this book. Some of these were listed as premiums or as for-sale products in Larkin catalogs; some were not. To distinguish between them, this chapter is divided into two parts. The first part will deal with previously unmentioned Buffalo Pottery products that were offered by Larkin as premiums or for sale. The second part will take up the articles not ever offered in the Larkin catalogs.

PART 1

In general, more information is available about items that were listed in the Larkin catalogs. The mere act of listing automatically provides an item with a date even if an actual specimen of the piece has not come to light. The catalog listing also provides certain descriptive details.

DINNERWARE

The first Buffalo Pottery dinnerware that appeared in the Larkin premium catalogs was the Lamare and Modjeska dinner and tea sets. These appeared originally in the catalog of April, 1904. Subsequently, many other patterns were offered. It is interesting to note that upon the receipt of ten cents in stamps, the Larkin Company would ship free of charge a sample individual butter dish so that the customer could examine the pattern he had chosen before ordering the entire set. Dinner sets were available in various assortments, ranging from fifty-three to one hundred and twelve pieces, according to the customer's preference.

All the early dinnerware (before World War I) was semivitreous china, and each piece was marked with the pottery name (Ill. 20), but very few early dinner sets were dated. The name of the pattern, however, appeared on the reverse side of many pieces. Later dinnerware (after World War I) was no longer marked "Buffalo Pottery," but "Buffalo China"; and most of the pieces carried the date as well as the trademark. At the end of the war (the pottery had suspended production of china for civilian use during the war), ware was again made for the Larkin Company catalogs, and this was all vitrified china, the finest quality the pottery had ever produced.

Given below are the names of the dinnerware patterns, the years in which they were offered in the catalogs, and details about them taken from the catalog descriptions. It is not known whether any of this ware was offered through other distribution outlets of the pottery.

Lamare, 1904 through 1908:
Sprays of poppies, choice of dove, dark blue, green, or brown. Embossed work in pure gold.

Modjeska, 1904 through 1909:
Pink roses or blue forget-me-nots. Pure gold trim.

Wild Poppy, 1905 through 1908:
Borders of wild poppies in olive green.

Bonrea (named for Louis Bown and William Rea), 1905 through 1916:
Ornate scroll border in myrtle green with pure gold trim.
(See Ills. 314 and 319.)

Old Blue Willow Ware, 1905 through 1917.

Color Band (Ill. 315), 1909 through 1910:
Plain with wide color band and two pure gold lines bordering each piece. Comes in apple green, turquoise, or maroon.

Miana (Ill. 314), 1909 through 1910:
Border pattern of Persian design in Oriental colors, dark and light blue and green predominating.

Kenmore (Ill. 315), 1909 through 1911:
Art Nouveau and floral border in green decor, illuminated in gold and gold trim.

Buffalo (Ill. 315), 1909 through 1914:
Sprays of roses and altheas in natural colors. Full gold trim.

Maple Leaf (Ill. 314), 1909 through 1914:
Small border of green maple leaves and pink flowers with full gold trim.

Princess (Ill. 314), 1909 through 1914:
Green floral border with full gold trim.

Seneca (Ill. 315), 1909 through 1914:
Border of flowers. Choice of green or dark blue. Gold handles and embossed work.

Tea Rose (Ill. 314), 1909 through 1914:
Small border of pink roses and green leaves with full gold trim.

Gold Band (Ill. 314), 1909 through 1915:
Plain white with a wide pure gold band.

Forget-Me-Not (Ills. 315 and 317), 1909 through 1917:
Forget-me-nots in border pattern with full gold trim.

Florence Rose, 1910:
Double border of pink roses and green leaves with edges and embossed work in gold.

Gold Lace Border, 1911 through 1914:
Gold border in a lace design. Edges and embossed work in gold.

Pluto, 1911 through 1916:
Wide border of pink roses and green leaves, in natural colors. Edges and embossed work in pure gold.

Queen, 1911 through 1917:
Narrow border of pink roses and green leaves in natural colors, edges and embossing in gold.

Minerva, 1913 through 1916:
  Sprays of pink roses and spring beauties. Full gold trim.
Vienna (Ill. 318), 1915:
  Designs in dark blue underglaze. Full gold trim.
Vassar, 1915 through 1916:
  Designs in conventional dark green underglaze.
Empress, 1915 through 1917:
  Green conventional border. Full gold trim.
Fern Rose, 1915 through 1917:
  Border design of small pink roses and green leaves with full gold trim.
Wild Rose, 1915 through 1917:
  Wild roses and spring flowers in natural colors with gold trim.
Gold Line, 1916 through 1917:
  Plain white, decorated with two narrow gold lines.
Rosebank, 1917:
  Wide border of pink roses and green leaves in natural colors. Edges traced in gold.
Spray Decor Tea Set, 1919 through 1920:
  Vitreous china. Sprays of pink roses. Very realistic and can hardly be told from hand-painting.
Blue Bird Tea Set (Ill. 320), 1919 through 1922:
  Vitreous china. Bluebird decor in full natural colors.
Bungalow, 1920 through 1921:
  Vitreous china. Fine latticework alternated with a fine floral decoration in red, green, or yellow. Blended and dotted beneath with little flowers. Full gold trim.
Dresden, 1920 through 1921:
  Vitreous china. Delicate pink roses and blue flowers intertwined and arranged in panels on a dainty ivory background. Edges and handles traced in coin gold.
Glendale, 1920 through 1921:
  Vitreous china. Comes in green, golden brown, turquoise blue. An unusual festoon design surrounding pink roses. Edges and handles traced in coin gold.
Pink Rose, 1920 through 1922:
  Vitreous china. Sprays of pink roses almost like hand-painting. Gold border.
Beverly (Ill. 316), 1921:
  Vitreous china. Conventional border interspersed with pink roses and green leaves. Pure coin gold handles.
Coin Gold Band, 1921:
  Vitreous china. Single band of coin gold $\frac{3}{16}$th inch wide. Pure gold handles.

The last two items represent the final offering of dinnerware made by Buffalo Pottery in the Larkin catalogs. They also were the most expensive dinnerware given as premiums—a customer had to make purchases worth $180 in order to obtain a 100-piece set of the dishes.

Some dinerware sets that the pottery made were never offered in the Larkin catalog. Among these were Lucerne, Arlington, Mandalay (Ill. 348), Indian Tree (Ill. 347), Japan (Ill. 343), and Bangor (Ill. 345). Japan and Bangor were both made in 1905, and both were hand-decorated in a variety of bright colors that gave them unusual attractiveness. The pottery issued Mandalay and Indian Tree in the mid-twenties, copying them from the patterns used on pieces produced by the famous English potteries. From the samples they have had an opportunity to compare, the authors believe that Buffalo Pottery articles in these two patterns are far superior to the English ware.

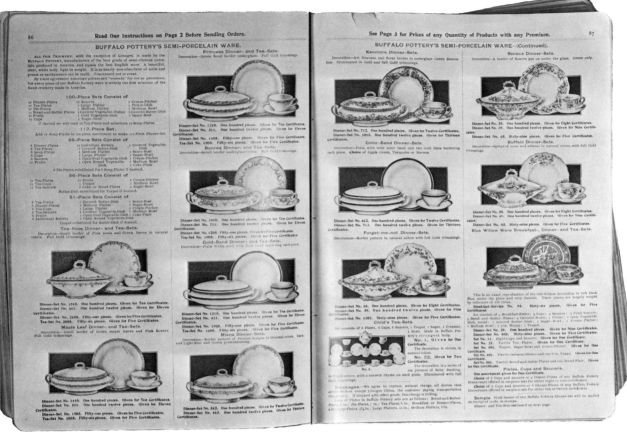

314. A page from the fall / winter catalog of 1909–1910 showing some of the dinnerware being offered at that time. *Courtesy of Harry H. Larkin, Jr.*

315. Facing catalog page to that shown in Ill. 314. Note the child's tea set at lower left. *Courtesy of Harry H. Larkin, Jr.*

316. Beverly pattern dinnerware, dated 1920, was decorated with pink roses, green leaves, and had coin gold handles and trim. *Courtesy of John A. Navagh.*

317. Forget-Me-Not dinner set was shown in Larkin catalogs from 1909 until 1917. *Courtesy of Schohn's Antiques.*

318. Vienna-pattern dinnerware, shown in the Larkin catalog in 1915, was decorated in blue with gold trim.

319. From 1905 until 1916, Larkin catalogs showed dinner sets in the gold-trimmed Bonrea pattern. Underglaze decoration was done in deep blue-green.

320. Bluebird pattern tea set, dated 1919. It was offered in Larkin catalogs from 1919 to 1922. The bluebirds are in natural colors.

321. Other pieces were also decorated in Bluebird pattern. *From left:* 8-inch personalized feeding dish, dated 1919; 5-inch butter tub, dated 1919; 8½-inch child's warming dish.

322. The first china made in Buffalo, November 4, 1904, was a hand-painted sugar and creamer. *Courtesy of the Vogel family.*

323. The bottom of the sugar bowl shown in Ill. 322. *Courtesy of the Vogel family.*

324. These pieces of hand-painted bone china are dated 1905. *Courtesy of the Vogel family.*

TOILET OR BATHROOM SETS

The period when toilet or bathroom sets were offered in the Larkin catalog was the period when indoor plumbing was still nonexistent in many parts of the country, especially in rural areas. The first Buffalo Pottery toilet set (the Cairo pattern) was shown in the Larkin catalog of January, 1905. Earlier catalogs had also offered a set in this pattern, but it was not manufactured by Buffalo Pottery. Cairo pattern toilet sets made by Buffalo Pottery were thereafter offered in almost every Larkin catalog (Ill. 325) until 1918, when they were apparently discontinued because of decreasing demand for them. The exact number is unknown, but there is little doubt that literally many thousands of Cairo sets were given away as premiums and sent to every part of the United States.

A complete eleven-piece toilet set consisted of a washbowl, pitcher, chamber pot with cover, a ribbed-bottom soap dish with cover, small pitcher for hot water, brush vase, shaving mug, and a slop jar with cover. If an eleven-piece set was not desired, a nine-piece set (minus the slop jar with cover) also was available. The Buffalo Pottery trademark was the only identification to be found on the bottom of these pieces.

Listed below are the bathroom sets offered in the Larkin catalogs, the years in which they were given, and sometimes the exact catalog description:

Cairo (Ill. 325), 1905 through 1916:
Decorated with a cluster of June roses in pink and yellow in natural green leaves with stems in a beautiful brown. Handles and edges traced in gold.
Chrysanthemum (Ill. 326), 1905 through 1910:
Same shape as Cairo sets, chrysanthemum sprays in green underglaze.
Tinted, 1906 through 1909:
Tinted from top to bottom and on panels with choice of pink, blue, or green. Full gold trim.
White and Gold (Ill. 325), 1906 through 1918:
"White body illuminated with gold."

325. The fall / winter catalog of 1915–1916 offered a choice of three designs in bathroom sets. *Courtesy of Harry H. Larkin, Jr.*

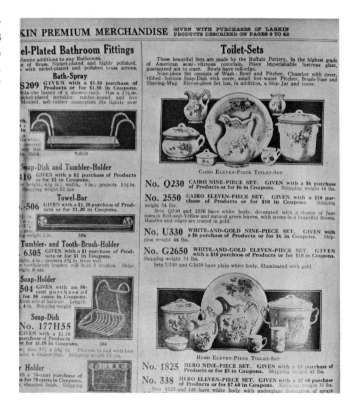

326. Part of a bathroom set in the Chrysanthemum pattern. Decoration was in green against a white body. *Courtesy of Schohn's Antiques.*

Hero (Ill. 325), 1913 through 1918:

"White body with underglazed decorations of sprays of green chrysanthemums."

Maple Leaf, 1914:

Small border of green maple leaves and pink flowers. Gold trim.

Princess, 1914:

Green floral border with gold trim.

Tea Rose, 1914 through 1918:

Clusters of yellow and pink roses on a white body with green leaves.

In 1917 and 1918, a large covered slop jar with bail handle was offered in the following patterns: Gold Band, Tea Rose, and Hero.

CHILDREN'S WARE

From 1904 through 1918, a twenty-two-piece child's tea set was offered. This consisted of six plates, six cups and saucers, a teapot with cover, a creamer, and sugar bowl. In the early catalogs the sets were decorated in an underglaze green floral decor. Later, sets were decorated with violets in natural colors (Ills. 315 and 328).

From 1906 through 1910, a child's twenty-two-piece tea set was given as a premium. This one was known as the Baby Bunting Set (Ill. 327). Each piece bore a nursery rhyme and also was decorated with a series of six Baby Bunting pictures in bright colors and trimmed in pure coin gold.

A child's 7¾-inch semivitreous china feeding dish decorated with various multicolor pictures of the Campbell Kids (Ill. 329) in the center and gold lines around the edges appeared in the catalogs of 1913 through 1918. Some of these dishes had the letters of the alphabet around the top rim. Most were engineered so that they could not be tipped easily. Feeding dishes are all marked "Buffalo Pottery," but none is dated. These were products to be sold, not premiums of the Larkin Company, and they cost fifty cents each. The purchase of one entitled the buyer to fifty cents' credit toward premiums; or, if he purchased one outright without premium credit, the cost was half the catalog price or twenty-five cents.

The authors also have in their collection the following items, of which no mention can be found in any Larkin catalog:

An infant's warming dish in the Blue Bird pattern (Ill. 321). This has a metal base into which hot water is poured to keep the food warm.

Another baby's feeding dish in the Blue Bird pattern (Ill. 321) that is similar in shape to the Campbell Kids dish.

Two white vitreous-china pitchers edged in gold, 3 and 5 inches tall respectively, that are decorated in multicolor with scenes from the Roosevelt Bears book (Ill. 330). These were done by applying a decal under the glaze. Both are marked "Buffalo China, 1919." We believe they are part of a child's cereal set.

327. The Baby Bunting tea set, which consisted of twenty-two pieces, was offered in Larkin catalogs from 1904 until 1918. The decal-applied scenes are in bright colors against a white body. *Courtesy of Mrs. Emil Klein.*

328. The child's tea set with violet decoration also consisted of twenty-two pieces. It was offered in the catalog from 1904 to 1918.

329. These undated Campbell Kids feeding dishes measure 7¾ inches and are decal-decorated in bright colors. They were offered by Larkin between 1913 and 1918.

330. Brightly colored scenes from *The Roosevelt Bears* decorate children's vitrified china pitchers 5 and 2¾ inches tall.

331. Three pieces from a six-piece children's cereal set, which was offered in the Larkin catalog in 1922. *Courtesy of Mr. and Mrs. Lawrence M. Nicholson.*

VASES

Three art pottery-type vases made of semivitreous china were listed in the premium catalogs of 1905. Their only identification was the Buffalo Pottery trademark:

Artistic Shape, 1905 through 1907:

"A decor of natural flowers in natural colors. Trimmed in gold. Six inches high."

Rococo, 1905 through 1907:

"Rococo design with a spray of clematis. Heavily traced in gold. Comes in a buff or apple green background. 10¼" high."

English Design, 1905 through 1909:

Decorated in sprays of flowers in original colors. 10" high.

SERVING PIECES

Chocolate Pot (Ill. 334), 1905 through 1908:

"9½" tall. Sprays of poppies in natural colors. Embossing and handles traced in gold. Choice of buff or apple green background." (Note: There apparently was some size variation, as the authors' chocolate pot in this pattern is 11" tall.)

Salad or Fruit Bowl (Ill. 332), 1905 through 1909:

"The decoration is a cluster of roses in their natural coloring against a green and pink background. Embossed work is traced in gold." This piece was described as being a "handsome sideboard piece, 10¾" in diameter."

Cake Plate (12") and **Celery Tray** (11¾"), (Ill. 332), 1905 through 1910:

The same decor as the salad bowl.

Oatmeal Set, 1905 through 1910:

Three-piece set consisting of one bowl, one cream pitcher, and one plate. A set of six bowls was also available. "The decoration was sprays of roses, lilacs and forget-me-nots in natural colors. Edges and handles were traced in gold."

Cracker Jar, 1905 through 1912:

Sprays of poppies in natural colors. Embossing and handles done in gold. Buff or green background. 5½" high.

Fruit Set, 1905 through 1912:

"Consists of 8½" diameter fruit bowl and six saucers. Each has a different center decoration of natural fruit with sprays of flowers on the sides."

Chocolate Pot (Ill. 335), 1908 through 1911:

New design. 11" high. Sprays of wild roses in natural colors. Handle and embossed work done in gold. Choice of buff or Flemish green background. Chocolate cups and saucers to match the chocolate pot were never mentioned, and so we assume none were ever made.

Egg Cup Set, 1909:

Six double cups to a set, in pure white.

Tea Pot (Ill. 336)

One of the most ingenious and practical items ever produced and patented by the pottery was shown in the Larkin fall/winter catalog of 1915–1916. This piece was known as the "Tea Ball Tea Pot." It was vitrified china decorated under the glaze in a blue floral pattern called Argyle. A nickel-silver and silver-plated tea ball was suspended permanently, with a chain, under the lid. Filled with tea leaves, this could be lowered into the water for the tea to infuse, and raised upward when the brewing was complete. The cover of this pot can be lifted off, but is so constructed as not to fall off no matter at what angle the teapot is held. The pot made six cups of "perfect" tea. These teapots were sold as a Larkin product for two dollars; if premium credit was not desired, the price was only one dollar. A teapot in the authors' collection is marked "Buffalo Pottery" and "Argyle," and bears the date 1914. The word "China" also appears above the buffalo. This is one of the rare instances where a piece of vitreous china was marked "Buffalo Pottery" and not "Buffalo China."

China Butter Tub, 1916 through 1919:

A pretty 5-inch butter tub of translucent vitrified china decorated with delicate apple-blossom design. Edges and handles were decorated with coin gold lines. Drainer was a separate piece decorated with a coin-gold line. This was a product to be sold for eighty-five cents; not a premium.

332.   Serving dishes, shown in Larkin catalogs from 1905 until 1910, were decorated with clusters of roses in natural coloring against a pink and green background with gold tracery. Salad or fruit bowl at left is 10¾ inches in diameter; cake plate is 12 inches. The celery tray (front) is 11¾ inches long.

333.   Plate (9¼ inches) with deep blue-green border and colorful cluster of roses was probably made around 1905.

335. Gold trim and sprays of wild roses in natural color against a buff background decorate this 11-inch chocolate pot. It was shown in the catalogs from 1908 until 1911. No chocolate cups came with it. *Courtesy of Mrs. Robert Vidler.*

336. The teaball teapot in Argyle Pattern is dated 1914. Decoration is blue against a white body.

334. A 11½-inch chocolate pot decorated with sprays of poppies in color against a green background. It was shown in Larkin catalogs from 1905 until 1911.

CUSPIDORS

Cuspidors were shown only in the 1905 catalog. "The decoration is sprays of chrysanthemums in bluish green applied under the glaze. Embossings traced with gold."

PART 2

In the twenties and thirties, the Larkin Company turned almost exclusively to imported china for premium use because it was less expensive to buy the imported than to buy that made by Buffalo Pottery. As a result of this change, Buffalo Pottery thereafter turned to the manufacture and design of exclusive hotel and institutional ware.

The articles discussed in the remainder of this chapter are either nonpremium Buffalo Pottery items not mentioned previously or special items the pottery made during later years.

DRINKING SETS (Ill. 337)

Drinking sets that consisted of six mugs with handles and a tall tankard were made by Buffalo Pottery but never shown as either premiums or products for sale by the Larkin Company. They came in a variety of designs, colors, and shapes. The earliest sets known, semivitreous with overglaze decoration, are marked "Buffalo Pottery." Although they are undated, the authors believe they were made from 1905 to 1908. Some were decorated with decal pictures of the Old Friar drinking ale on one side of the mug and with roses on the other side. Others bore pictures of Indians. Later on, probably in the 1930's, tankard sets with the Friar picture were made of vitrified china, on Colorido, Rouge, Café au Lait, Lune, and Ye Old Ivory bodies.

Also made in the thirties on these body colors were Tom and Jerry Sets (Ill. 352) consisting of a large punch bowl with a dozen drinking mugs. "Tom and Jerry" in English script was applied under the glaze to each piece.

337.   Drinking set in green, with multicolor figures, was probably made between 1905 and 1908. It came in other colors and with various friar scenes. Tankard-type pitcher is 14 inches tall. Mugs are 5½ inches. *Courtesy of Agnes E. Masters.*

MULTIFLEURE (Ill. 338)

In 1925 the pottery brought out dinnerware with a marbled look that was the result of a deliberately incomplete blending of their five basic colored clays: Colorido, Rouge, Café au Lait, Lune, and Ye Old Ivory. The colored clays were mixed at random—without any specific plan; thus, the colors were not merely a surface application but ran completely through the body of a piece. The pottery devised a French-sounding name for this vitrified ware—Multifleure—and most pieces are clearly marked with it: "Buffalo China, Multifleure."

A number of hotels and restaurants chose dinnerware of Multifleure, and it was also molded into vases of various sizes and shapes. All Multifleure specimens are quite scarce today. In the absence of definite records, it is believed that production of this ware was rather short-lived.

TURKEY SET (Ill. 340)

In 1937 Buffalo Pottery designed and made a special set of dishes for use during the Thanksgiving and Christmas seasons. This complete service, which became known as the Turkey Set, was made in a very limited quantity. Colorido or yellow was the background color. Each piece was decorated with a harvest scene around the border; the large rectangular platter had, in addition, a turkey in the center.

The Turkey Set was vitreous china. The scenes were transfer-applied prints hand-decorated in natural colors; Ralph Stuart created them. The set bears no date, but is identified by the mark on the bottom: Colorido Ware, Buffalo China.

NATURAL WOOD DESIGN (Ill. 339)

In 1939 a limited quantity of pieces was made with a wood-grained effect complete with knots. These pieces were items that are generally made of real wood—both large and individual salad bowls. The Buffalo Pottery specimens were made of vitrified china, the wood-grain effect being produced by applying natural wood colors with a brush. These pieces were marked "Natural Wood Design."

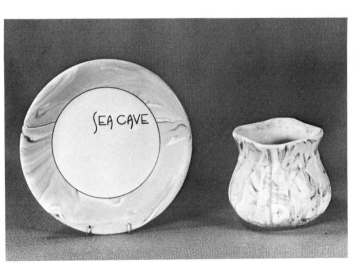

338. The 7½-inch bowl at left, from the service made for the Sea Cave Restaurant, is a good example of Multifleure Lamelle. The little 4-inch vase at right is entirely of Multifleure.

339. Five-inch bowl in Natural Wood Design, which was applied by hand.

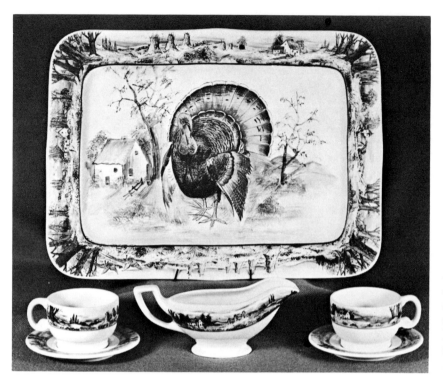

340. The Turkey Dinner set, designed by Ralph Stuart, was hand-
decorated in bright autumn colors
on a Colorido body. The handsome
large platter measures 18½ by 13¼
inches. *Courtesy of Mr. and Mrs.
Barry J. Rodgers.*

PORTLAND VASE (Ill. 341)

For three hundred years, one of the most admired works of art has been the
famous "Barberini Vase," which was discovered early in the seventeenth century.
This masterpiece in glass was so named because it was one of the outstanding
pieces in the collection of the celebrated Barberini family. Later it also became
known, as it still is today, as the Portland Vase. (It became part of the famous
collection of the Duchess of Portland in 1785.)

It was to Josiah Wedgwood, in the latter part of the eighteenth century, that
the Portland Vase first served as an inspiration for reproduction. His replicas
in china, sold to collectors in limited quantities at prohibitive prices, were the
forerunner of the famous Wedgwood China. Wedgwood made seven copies of
the Portland Vase, one of which he bestowed on a very dear friend, Joshua
Mayer, who was also a notable potter of that day.

In 1908, the vase given to Mayer came to the United States as the property
of Ernst Mayer of Beaver Falls, Pennsylvania, from whom William Rea had
learned the pottery trade. Through Rea's efforts, the vase was brought to
Buffalo and recast in plaster, but further work was delayed for a long period.
Finally the task of reproduction was entrusted to an assistant, and in 1925—
after numerous experiments—he succeeded in producing an exquisite counterpart
of the original Portland Vase (Ill. 341). The assistant's name was George H.
Wood; he was obviously a potter and chemist of considerable talent. Approximately six of the Portland Vases were produced at this time. However, in 1946,
President Gould used the original plaster cast and reproduced a limited number
of the vases by the Art Lamelle Process. Although these were good reproductions,
they did not compare in quality to the ones Wood produced earlier.

From the same clays used in producing the Portland Vase, George Wood
created and designed a number of blue-and-white Wedgwood-like medallions,
which were given to various friends and employees. Among the subjects presented
on the medallions were Liszt, Beethoven, Wagner, Verdi, Elbert Hubbard, George

Washington, Thomas Jefferson, and John D. Larkin (Ill. 342). The Field Museum in Chicago has one of these medallions in its collection.

Some of the less familiar items of Buffalo Pottery have been discussed in this chapter, but the authors feel certain that many more are extant and awaiting discovery. After our many years of research, we still come across pieces that we did not know existed. For example, included in a lot of dishes recently purchased from an old local estate was a boat-shaped serving piece (Ill. 354) about 4½ inches long marked "Buffalo China" and dated 1918. This was indeed a unique find. The entire inside of the piece is highly iridescent—the only iridescent item made by Buffalo Pottery that we have ever seen. In fact, we did not know that ware of this type had ever been made by the pottery. This little piece is decorated outside with hand-painted blue forget-me-nots and green leaves against a pale yellow background; the edges are trimmed in gold.

How many novelty-type items the pottery may have produced is unknown. A few of them are pictured in this book—cowboy-hat ashtrays and snail-shaped toothpick holders, both shown in Ill. 354, and canister sets (Ill. 353). But the pottery is known also to have put out corn dishes, candleholders, bud vases, additional mugs, and a variety of odd serving pieces—all in various colors and patterns.

In any case, it should not be concluded that the articles mentioned and/or pictured in this book represent the entire production of Buffalo Pottery.

341. The famous Portland Vase as reproduced at Buffalo Pottery in very limited numbers. Height is 8 inches. The vase was made in 1925 and again in 1946. *Courtesy of Harry H. Larkin, Jr.*

342. Identical to deep blue and white jasperware is this oval medallion (7¼ by 6 inches) portrait of John D. Larkin. It is signed "Wood" and dated 1925. *Courtesy of Mrs. Walter B. Robb.*

343. Dated 1906, this 10¼-inch colorful plate in Japan pattern is hand-decorated.

344. Ornate hand-decorated 10-inch plate with considerable gold tracing is dated 1906.

345. This hand-decorated plate is the same size and date as the one in Ill. 344. Pattern is Bangor. (See also color plate C1.)

346. Hand-decorated plate in Statler pattern. It measures 11¼ inches and is dated 1910. *Courtesy of Winnie Kurtz.*

347. Indian Tree dinnerware pattern was copied from the similar English pattern around 1930. The decoration was done by applying a brightly colored decal under the glaze. The pattern was made against various background colors.

348. Mandalay pattern was made on various colored backgrounds, the brightly colored decal decoration being applied under the glaze. Circa 1930.

349. Nine-inch, circa-1930 plate is hand-decorated in bright colors. Body is Rouge Lamelle (pink with white center).

350. Plate (9 inches) with Colorido Lamelle body is decorated with English hunting scene, applied under the glaze as a brightly colored decal. Circa 1930.

351. Punch bowl with Fallowfield Hunt scenes should not be confused with Deldare. Here the hand-decorator scenes are on a Colorido body. Bowl is 14½ inches high, 9 inches in diameter. Circa 1930. *Courtesy of Mr. and Mrs. Robert L. Crane.*

352. Tom and Jerry set has black lettering on a Colorido body. Bowl is 11¼ inches across, 6½ inches high.

353. Cannister sets in a blue-and-white floral pattern were made at the pottery in 1906. These two pieces are only a small part of the set. *Courtesy of Mr. and Mrs. Charles Spranger.*

354. Novelty items made at Buffalo Pottery. *Top row* (from left): nut dish, highly iridescent inside, hand-painted with forget-me-nots, dated 1918; clam-shaped white ashtray with gold trim; cowboy hat ashtray in Blue Lune. *Lower row* (from left): white snail-shaped toothpick holder; 4-inch white chocolate cup with gold trim, flanked by vitrified china handles made for silverware for the Biltmore Hotel; candleholder (came in various body colors) made for the Hotel Commodore.

355. Novelty white-bodied mugs decorated in varied colors were made in the pottery's early days. (Height, 4½ inches.)

356. R. Stuart signed this 10-inch plate titled "Fisher Village in Holland," and dated 1912. The decoration is in beautiful shades of blue. *Courtesy of Frances Bryan Murray.*

357. Size, date, and signature are the same as for the plate shown in Ill. 356. The plate shown here, however, is hand-decorated blue and white that resembles Delft. On the back it is labeled "Aonia Ware." *Courtesy of Frances Bryan Murray.*

358. Hand-decorated with geraniums in a variety of colors, this 3¾-inch rose bowl is dated 1907.

359. Ten-inch vase in blue and white Delft-like decoration is an early, undated piece. *Courtesy of Mr. and Mrs. Ralph Stuart.*

360. Jumbo blue and white cup measures 6¾ inches across, 3¼ inches high. This is an early undated piece. Reverse side pictures a boy fishing. Jumbo-size cup was also made in Blue Willow pattern. *Courtesy of Mrs. Walter B. Robb.*

361. Large white bone china teapot has gold handle, spout, and trim. This ware was made exclusively for the John D. Larkin family, and Mrs. Larkin's name appears on it in gold. This is another piece marked on the bottom "First China Made in Buffalo"—but the date here is 1905. (See Ill. 322.) *Courtesy of Mrs. Walter B. Robb.*

362.   In 1909, the pottery used Dr. Syntax scenes in blue, similar to those on Staffordshire ware. Rectangular platter 14 by 11 inches shows "Dr. Syntax Advertisement for a
Wife." *Courtesy of the Buffalo and Erie County Historical Society.*

363.   This 9-inch plate offers another example
of a Dr. Syntax scene in blue. Like the platter
in Ill. 362, it is dated 1909. The same scene—
"Dr. Syntax disputing his bill with the Landlady"—also appears on the 1911 Emerald Deldare teapot in Ill. 179. Not only is there no
mistaking the color difference between the
Syntax blue pieces and Emerald Deldare; the
blue pieces have typical Clews floral borders,
whereas the Emerald Deldare borders are always Art Nouveau in character. It is also interesting to note the variation in minor details
within the scene itself. *Courtesy of the Buffalo
and Erie County Historical Society.*

364. Emerald green china vase is decorated with sterling silver overlay. Vase measures 8 inches and is dated 1910. *Courtesy of the Vogel family.*

365. Vase (8½ inches) with cobalt blue body has turquoise decoration around the neck and heavy gold encrustation over the entire vase. Inside is also gold. Circa 1910. *Courtesy of the Vogel family.*

366. An unusually handsome 9-inch plate made around 1910. Hand decoration is in a variety of colors on an ivory body, the center figure being entirely in pure gold. *Courtesy of the Vogel family.*

367. The girl in the center of the 9-inch scalloped plate is hand-painted. Background is gray, highlighted with a good deal of gold trim. This is an early piece. *Courtesy of the Vogel family.*

368. Blue and white plate titled "The Land of Memory" is dated 1913. Plate measures 10½ inches. *Courtesy of the Vogel family.*

369. This 9½-inch hand-decorated plate is one of a series of automobiling plates. It was painted and signed by R. Stuart. *Courtesy of the Vogel family.*

370. Plate from the set of monogrammed dinnerware made for the personal use of Louis Bown. Pieces are dated 1918. Monogram is in pure gold; border is maroon. *Courtesy of Frances Bryan Murray.*

Commercial Service Clients

The names that follow were taken from old Buffalo Pottery workbooks containing emblems, crests, and decorative designs created for clients. Sometimes the client's name was incorporated into a drawing; sometimes it was written alongside the drawing; but sometimes the drawing gave no clue whatsoever to the identity of the client for whom it had been made. A few drawings were dated, and these dates are shown after the name, in parentheses, in the list given here, which—incidentally—contains only a small fraction of Buffalo Pottery's commercial clients, since the majority of the drawings were unidentified.

Unfortunately, in many cases where the client's name was indicated, it appeared only in part and/or without an address. Since the list is a lengthy one, and many of the firms on it may be long gone from the commercial scene, the authors have not attempted to research further into these names and addresses. Doubtless, the older reader will recognize the names of firms once active in his own locality. Of course, many of these restaurants, hotels, clubs, and so on, may still be in existence.

The authors have seen countless handsome pieces from commercial services, specimens any collector would be proud to own. However attractive and interesting these may be, though, not all commercial tableware made by Buffalo Pottery was so fine and artistic. Some was certainly relatively plain, heavy, and perhaps strictly utilitarian. Hence, the collector may have to do a bit of searching to find examples of the better-quality services and designs that appeal to him. This list, as far as the authors know, includes no clients who chose from stock patterns, and none that date from the post-1940 period, and so it should be helpful to the searcher.

A. F. & A. M. Masons
Adam's House (1917)
Adelphia Coffee Shop,
    Philadelphia, Pa.
Agwi Lines (1928)
Airport Café
Alaska Steamship Co.,
    Seattle, Wash.
Alden Grange #1130
Alexian Brothers Hospital
All state institutions, Salem, Ore.
Alpha Chi Rho
Alpha Epsilon Phi
Alpha Gamma Rho,
    Cornell University, Ithaca, N.Y.
Alpha Kappa Lambda

Alpha Zeta, Cornell University,
    Ithaca, N.Y.
Alpine Restaurant, Ithaca, N.Y.
American Café
American Export Lines
American Hotel Association
American Mail Line
American War Mothers
Ann Maude Cafeteria,
    Oklahoma City, Okla.
Arctic Club, Seattle, Washington
Argyle Hotel
Army & Navy Club, Manila, P.I.
Arrowhead Springs, Calif.
Astor Hotel, New York City
Atlanta Hotel, Atlanta, Ga.

Atlantic Coastline Railroad,
    Washington, D.C.
Avery's Inn
Automobile Club of Buffalo

B.P.O.E. #211, Jersey City, N.J.
Bakersfield Lodge, B.P.O.E.
Baltimore and Ohio Railroad
Baltimore Dairy Lunch—
    J.A. Whitcomb
Bar 37—Guest Ranch
Barcalo, Buffalo, N.Y.
Battleship *Oregon* (1933)
Bausch & Lomb Optical Co.,
    Buffalo, N.Y.

Baylor University,
    Waco, Dallas, and Houston, Tex.
Beefsteak Barnie
Belle River, Kansas City
Bellevue-Stratford,
    Philadelphia, Pa.
Belmont School
Bendix Aviation Corp,
    South Bend, Ind.
Bettner Camp
Birchwood Arbor
Biscayne Bay Lodge #124
    F. & A.M.
Bismarck Garden (1917)
Bismarck Hotel (1917),
    Chicago, Ill.
Blackstone Hotel, Fort Worth, Tex.
Blessed's
Board of Education,
    Rochester, N.Y.
Boston City Club
Boston Oyster House
Boy Scouts of America,
    National Council, New York City
Bradley Transportation Company
Brae Lodge
Brevoort Hotel
British Home (1925)
Brooklyn College
Brown Derby, Los Angeles, Calif.
Buffalo Athletic Club, Buffalo, N.Y.
Buffalo Chamber of Commerce
    (1917)
Buffalo Club, Buffalo, N.Y.
Buffalo Consistory Valley of
    Buffalo, N.Y.
Buffalo General Hospital,
    Buffalo, N.Y.
Buffalo Launch Club
Buffalo Trap & Field Club (1928)
Buffalo Tennis & Squash Club
    (1927)
Burbridge Hotel, Jacksonville, Fla.
Burt Cottage

C.D. & G.B. Transit Co.
C.R.I. Railroad
Café Milano
California Club
California Transportation Company
Calumet Club of New York
Camp Cheno
Canadian National System
Canandaigua Pale Ale
Candlelight House, St. Louis, Mo.
Caroline Mission
Casa de Alex (school club)
Castle Square Hotel (1917),
    Boston, Mass.

Cedarbrook Country Club
Centenary Church
Charles W. Cushman F. & A.M.
    #879
Chatham Bars Inn
Chesapeake and Ohio Hospital,
    Huntington, W. Va.
Chesapeake and Ohio Railroad,
    Covington, Ky.
Chicago, Burlington & Quincy
    Railroad, the "Zephyr"
Chicago, Milwaukee & St. Paul
    Railroad
Chicago Northwestern Line
Chief Lunch
Children's Orthopedic Hospital
    (1928)
Childs Hotel, Atlanta, Ga.
Childs Restaurant
China Royal
Christ Cella
Christ Church
Churchill Downs Race Track
Churchill Hotel, San Diego, Calif.
City Club of Utica, N.Y.
Clark Restaurant, Cleveland, Ohio
Club Palm
Club Palmetto
Cohasset Gulf Club
Colfox-Rebecca Lodge
College Inn (1925)
Collegium Lafayettense Veritas
    Liberabit
Collier Service Corporation
Colombo Café
Colonial Club, Princeton, N.J.
Colonial Steamship Lines
Columbian Club
Commercial Club of Fresno, Calif.
Commodore Hotel, New York City
Cooper Carlton, Chicago
Copper Teakettle
Country Club (1928),
    Camagüey, Cuba
Country Club, Westfield, N.J.
Country Club of Havana
Country Club of Reno, Nev.
Curriers Congregational Church

D. H. Community Center
Dadna Lines
Davenports
Davis Café (1926)
Day Lines
Daytona Beach Lodge #270
    A.F. & A.M.
Deaconess Society (1927)
Deco Restaurant, Buffalo, N.Y.
Delta Kappa Epsilon

Delta Sorority, Columbia, Mo.
Delta Tau Delta, Chicago, Ill.
Denver Country Club,
    Denver, Col.
Department of the Navy,
    Washington, D.C.
Dexter School
Dinty Moore's
Dold Packing Company
Dr. Cousin's Private Hospital,
    St. Barnabas
Drake Hotel, Chicago, Ill.
Dugans

Eagle Café (1923)
East Aurora Sun Diet Sanatorium
East Dallas Christian Church
Eastern Steamship Company,
    Boston, Mass.
Edgemoor
El Morocco
Electric Waffle Inn (1927)
Elkwood (1926)
Ellicott Club (1917)
El-Ro-Do
Emery Park Inn (1928)
Engineer's Club of Philadelphia
Epsilon Delta Chapter of
    Sigma Nu Fraternity
Eppler's (1925)
Erie Railroad, Jersey City, N.J.
Essex House
Evanston Golf Club

F. & A.M. Masons
Fairview Country Club
Fairview Grille
Fallen Leaf, Lake Tahoe
Faxon, Williams, & Faxon
Fenimore Country Club
Feyn Court Inn
Fidelity Trust Club
Fifty-fourth Brigade, Buffalo, N.Y.
5070 Clan Stuart, Buffalo, N.Y.
First Baptist Church of Valligo
    (1921), Calif.
Flamingo, Miami, Fla.
Floridian Hotel, Tampa, Fla.
Forest Service, Department of
    Agriculture, Washington, D.C.
Franklin Hospital,
    San Francisco, Calif.
Fredericka Home (1925)
Frisby Memorial Hospital
Furness Withy & Co., Limited
    (1928)

Gandy's Sea Food (1927),
    Buffalo, N.Y.

Garret Club
George Diamond Steaks (1927),
    Buffalo, N.Y.
Georgia's Place
Gettysburg College,
    Gettysburg, Pa.
Ginter Restaurant, Boston, Mass.
Girard College, Philadelphia, Pa.
Globe Dairy Lunch,
    Los Angeles, Calif.
Goodrich Steamship Lines (1926)
Governor Dummer Academy,
    Byfield, Mass.
Graduates Association
Great Northern Star (1917)
Greenbrier
Greenmill Gardens
Guam Hotel, Island of Guam

Hackensack Hospital
Hamilton Field
Harlem Valley Chapter IOES
    Home, New York City
Harmony Lodge, F. & A.M.
Harry Howell
Hart's Lunch, San Francisco, Calif.
Harvard Club of Boston
Harvard Club of New York
Haverford College
Healys (1917)
Heathman Hotel, Portland, Ore.
Henel's Kenmore Dairy,
    Buffalo, N.Y.
Henderson Hotel
Herbert's
Hillside Hotel
Hitching Post
Hobart
Hogi
Hollywood Tavern (1928)
Hotel Alabama
Hotel Apuloy
Hotel Atlantic
Hotel Baltimore (1926)
Hotel Belvidere
Hotel Bentley, Alexandria, La.
Hotel Bonta
Hotel Bossert, Brooklyn, N.Y.
Hotel Bristol
Hotel Carlyle (1926)
Hotel Charlotte, Charlotte, N.C.
Hotel Clark
Hotel Congress & Annex
Hotel Dempsey, Macon, Ga.
Hotel Dupont, Boston and Paris
Hotel Graystone, Buffalo, N.Y.
Hotel Henry (1917),
    Pittsburgh, Pa.
Hotel Henry Watterson

Hotel Hyde Park
Hotel Kimball
Hotel Klein
Hotel Lafayette (1926),
    Buffalo, N.Y.
Hotel Leighton, Los Angeles, Calif.
Hotel Lorraine
Hotel McAlpin, New York City
Hotel Martin, Milwaukee, Wis.
Hotel Melia, Ponce, P.R.
Hotel Morrison, Terrace Garden
Hotel Oceanic (1926)
Hotel Pfister
Hotel Putnam (1925),
    De Land, Fla.
Hotel Robert Fulton (1926)
Hotel Sherman (1916)
Hotel Statler
Hotel Thorndike, Boston, Mass.
Hotel Traymore, Montreal, Can.
Hotel Touraine
Hotel Utah
Hotel Vermont, Burlington, Vt.
Hotel Washington,
    Colón, P.R.
Huntington Restaurant,
    Portland, Me.
Huyler's

Idlewood
Illini Country Club,
    Springfield, Ill.
Illinois Masonic Hospital
Illinois Sugar Bowl, Peoria, Ill.
Indian Mills Country Club (1927)
International Business Machines
International Casino
International Mercantile Marine,
    New York City
Irondeqoit Country Club

Jack Dempsey's Restaurant,
    New York City
Jack Henry, Inc.
John's Rendezvous
Jol Sanitary Coffee Shop
Jolly Joan, San Francisco, Calif.
Jung Hotel, New Orleans, La.
Junior League

K of C, Brooklyn, N.Y.
Kane's
Keeler's Restaurant, Albany, N.Y.
Kappa Alpha Theta
Kappa Kappa Gamma
Kappa Sigma
Kenmore
Kennilworth of Los Angeles (1928)
King's Tea Garden

Knickerbocker Inn
Knollwood Country Club
Knowltson's
Kraft Cheese
Kugler's Restaurant,
    Philadelphia, Pa.

La Delfa
La Flor de Mexico (1925)
La Salle Hotel, Chicago, Ill.
Lackawanna Railroad
Lake Arrowhead Hotel,
    Lake Arrowhead, Calif.
Lakeside Hospital
Lakeview Tea Room,
    Duluth, Minn.
Lamda Chi Alpha
Lancey House
Langley's, Portland, Me.
Lang's
Laramie Golf Club (1925)
Larkin Co.
Laubes Old Spain (1925),
    Buffalo, N.Y.
Lawrence
Lee Sanitarium
Leeland Parker (1925)
Leo A. Schueneman Co.
Los Angeles Biltmore,
    Los Angeles, Calif.
Lido Hotel
Lil's Tavern, N. Hoosick, N.Y.
Lincoln Tavern (1923)
Loft Agency, Danbury, Conn.
Lord Strathcona's Horse R.C.—
    Sgts. Mess
Lorenzo's Restaurant (1933),
    Buffalo, N.Y.
Los Angeles City Club
Lou G. Segel, Inc.

M.K. & T. Railroad Co.,
    Kansas City, Mo.
Magnus Hotel
Mann's
Mare Island, San Francisco, Calif.
Markeen Hotel (1917)
Marlborough-Blenheim,
    Atlantic City, N.J.
"Mary Alice"
Masonic Temple (1925),
    Orlando, Fla.
Massachusetts General Hospital
    (1930), Boston, Mass.
Medford's
Medina Memorial Hospital
Merchant's Café
Mercy Hospital

Metro-Goldwyn-Mayer Studios,
    Culver City, Calif.
Metropolitan Café
Metropolitan Life Insurance
Midway Gardens
Monticello Steamship Co.
Morgan's Red Coach Inn,
    Closter, N.J.
Morrison's Cafeteria, Jackson, Miss.
Morrison's Cafeteria, Mobile, Ala.
Morton Chapter #164
Morton Lodge #204 F.A.M.
Mousan FLT #26
Mrs. Field's Place
Munson Steamship Lines

New Bedford College
New England Steamship Co.
New York Central Railroad,
    New York City
New York Guild Hospital
N.Y., N.H. & Hartford Railroad
    Co., Boston, Mass.
New York World's Fair 1939
Niagara Power
Niagara Sanitarium
Niagara University, Niagara 2, N.Y.
Nichols School
Nick's, Greenwich Village,
    New York, N.Y.
Normandy Hotel
North American Hotel
North Java Fire Co.
Norwegian Steamship Lines
Norwood Golf Club
Nypen Club

Oakgrove Café
O'Henry Hotel, Greensboro, N.C.
Old Cathedral (1925), Chicago, Ill.
Old Heidelberg
Old Toll Gate (1930)
Olive Chapter #325 (1925)
174th Infantry, Buffalo, N.Y.
174th Regiment
135th Infantry, Minneapolis, Minn.
Ontario Club (1927)
Oregon Agricultural College
Oriole Cafeterias, Baltimore, Md.
Otis & Stans
Oxford Hotel, Denver, Col.

Pacific Steamship Company
Pacific Union Club,
    San Francisco, Calif.
Palace Hotel, San Francisco, Calif.
Palace Hotel, Shanghai, China
Panama R.R. Steamship Co.
Paredone Golf Club

Paris Hospital (1933)
Park Central Hotel, New York City
Park Club
Park Lane, Buffalo, N.Y.
Parkway Hotel
Patrons of Husbandry
Pell's (1927)
Peninsular & Occidental Steamship
    Co.
Penn Athletic Club,
    Philadelphia, Pa.
Pennsylvania State University,
    University Park, Pa.
Pennsylvania Railroad
Père Marquette Hotel
Père Marquette Railroad,
    Ludington, Mich.
Père Marquette S.S. Lines
Phi Delta Theta
Phi Epsilon Phi
Phi Kappa Psi, Calif.
Phillips Exeter Academy,
    Exeter, N.H.
Photographers' Association of
    America
Pickwick
Pier 33
Pilot Sea Food (1933)
Pinehurst Department Store (1917)
Polo Club
Post Tavern (1926)
Puerto Rico Lines (1927)
Puget Sound Hotels
Pulako's
Pullman Co.

Rainier National Park,
    Tacoma, Wash.
Rapputak
Red Coach Inn, Niagara Falls, N.Y.
Red D Line
Regina Council, K of C
Reno Country Club
Republic Café
Restaurant Madrillon
Richfield Springs Lodge #482,
    F.A.M.
Richmond Hospital
Rich's, Atlanta, Ga.
Rideau Club
Rock Island Streamliner
Royal Apartments
Royal Montreal Golf Club (1923)
Roycroft Inn
Rudill's Coffee Shop

S.S. *Leviathan*, U.S. Lines,
    New York City
S.S. *Manhattan*, U.S. Lines,
    New York City

St. Andrew's Scottish Society,
    Buffalo, N.Y.
St. Boniface
St. Clair's, Inc., Boston, Mass.
St. John's Ladies Aid
St. John's Lodge #17
St. Luke's Hospital, Denver, Col.
St. Matthew's Church
St. Peter's
Salvation Army
San Diego & Arizona Railroad
    (1923)
San Jose Hospital, San Jose, Calif.
Sandy Yacht Club
Saratoga Tavern
Saturn Club
Savannah Lines (1923)
Savarin's Restaurant,
    Philadelphia, Pa.
Savern Restaurants, New York City
Savoy Café (1926)
Schaber's Cafeteria,
    Los Angeles, Calif.
Scherer's Lunch
Schenplein's, Montgomery, N.Y.
Schroeder Hotels, Chicago, Ill.
Sea Cave
Seminole Café
Seminole Inn
Shackamaxon
Shaftil's
Sherry's, New York City
Ship's Gallery
Shoal Water
Sigma Chi Nu, Alfred, N.Y.
Silver Tip Ranch
Slough Creek
Smoke Tree Ranch,
    Palm Springs, Calif.
Sociedad Española, P.R.
Solari's, New Orleans, La.
South Shore Country Club
Southern California Edison Com-
    pany
Southern Pacific Railroad,
    San Francisco, Calif.
Southern Railroad Co.,
    Washington, D.C.
Southside Swedish Club
Standard Oil Company of Havana
Standard Oil of New York
State of New York
Stein's (1920), Buffalo, N.Y.
Stevens College Fraternity,
    Hoboken, N.J.
Stuart (1923), Springfield, Ill.
Stuyvesant Hotel (1923),
    Buffalo, N.Y.
Sulgrave's Club

Sussman Volk Delicatessen
Syke's

Tahoe Tavern, Lake Tahoe, Calif.
Tenafly School Cafeteria,
Tenafly, N.J.
The Addison
The Admiral Line, P.S.S. Co.
The Ahwahnee, Yosemite Park,
Calif.
The Allerton (1923)
The Biltmore, Los Angeles, Calif.
The Castilla, St. Louis, Mo.
The Cawthorn
The Chanticleer
The Commander Hotel
The Dunes Club, Narraganset, R.I.
The Eastbourne (1925),
Atlantic City, N.J.
The Ellicott Club
The Ferguson
The Fo' Cas'le
The Genesee
The Gotham, New York City
The Hargrave (1923)
The Homestead
The Irving (1927)
The Lotus Club (1927),
New York City
The Majestic
The Marion
The Masquers
The Masons
The Mayflower, Washington, D.C.
The Moraine (1925),
Highland Park, Ill.
The Oasis
The Osage Sweet
The Otesage
The Pittsburgh Davis
The Red Rooster
The Rockett
The St. Charles
The Shelbourne
The Stockton
The Tacoma
The Trocadero

The Union League,
Philadelphia, Pa.
The Vernon Inn
Theta Delta
Theta Upsilon Omega
Thomasville Shooting Club
Thorwald (1926)
Tom's Dixie Kitchen,
Manila, P.I.
Tony's Gengia's Atlantic Lobster
House
Topa-Topa Lodge (1930)
Topeka Hill School, Topeka, Kan.
Traymore Cafeteria (1926),
Montreal, Can.
Trim-Too
Turtle Lake Club (1930)
Tuxedo Memorial Hospital
Twentieth Century Limited
250 Coast Artillery

Union League Club, Chicago, Ill.
Union Pacific Club
Union Pacific Railroad
U.S. American Legion
U.S. Army Medical Department
U.S. Bureau of Fisheries,
Washington, D.C.
U.S. Forest Service, Citadel, Mont.
U.S. Grant Hotel
U.S. Lines
U.S. Marine Corps (1922)
U.S. Military Academy,
West Point, N.Y.
U.S. Naval Academy,
Annapolis, Md.
U.S. Public Health Service
U.S. Shipping Board
Unity Inn
University Club (1930)
University Lunch (1917)
University of Buffalo
University of California,
Berkeley, Calif.
University of Illinois
University of Maine, Orono, Me.

University of Redlands,
Redlands, Calif.

Vacaville Lodge #134, F. & A.M.
Vassil's Brothers

WEBR Radio Station, Buffalo, N.Y.
Waldorf-Astoria
Waldorf Lunch (1917)
Waldorf Systems, Inc.,
Boston, Mass.
Walters of Brookline
Warburton House,
Philadelphia, Pa.
Warm Springs Foundation,
Warm Springs, Ga.
Washington Boulevard Hospital
Western Stores Company
Westminster Church
Westover Hotel
White Cafeterias
White Cotton Hotel
White Sulphur Springs
Wianno Club, Wianno, Mass.
Wildroot
Willard Hotel, Washington, D.C.
Wm. Filenes Company,
Boston, Mass.
Willworth Cafeteria,
Framingham, Mass.
Wilshire Golf Club
Wilson Inn
Women's City Club, Boston, Mass.
Women's Club of Hollywood
Women's Gettysburg College
Wongs, London, England
Woodfoods Club
Wranglers Fraternity
Wyomissing Club
Ye Bullpen Inn

Y.M.C.A.
Y.W.C.A.
Yellowstone Park Hotel,
Gardiner, Mont.

Zion Mission Church (1923)

Glossary

Art Nouveau: Style of decoration and design popular between about 1885 and 1910. In America, it was evident mostly in the decorative field, and mainly involved ornament. Art Nouveau is characterized by swirling lines, curved forms, and profuse use of such curvilinear motifs as flowers, vines, seaweed, and elongated female bodies with long flowing hair.

Art Pottery: Articles made of clay that are unique in decoration or form.

Biscuit, or Bisque, Kiln: Oven in which pottery is fired before it has been glazed.

Bone China: Vitreous, translucent pottery containing bone ash. It is delicate in appearance but very strong.

Café Au Lait: Trade name used by Buffalo Pottery for tan solid-body vitreous china.

Casting: Shaping a fluid material (which subsequently solidifies) by pouring it into a mold.

Ceramics: All products made from clay.

China: Glazed or unglazed vitreousware used for tableware, sanitary articles, and artware.

Clay: A natural material characterized by its plasticity, either as it comes from the clay pit or after being pulverized and mixed with water.

Coin Gold: Gold of the purity legalized for use in coins.

Colorido Ware: Buffalo Pottery trade name for yellow solid-body vitreous china.

Copper Cylinder Decoration: Design applied to an object by means of a specially prepared paper that has been passed over a revolving drum on which the design was first engraved. In other words, ink or color applied to the design on the drum is transferred by means of the special paper to a third object.

Decalcomania: Process of transferring designs or pictures to glass, china, and various other surfaces by means of a specially prepared paper. Known as "decal" for short. Decalcomania, which is really only one of the types of transfer printing, usually is done in more than one color.

Decorating, or Muffled, Kiln: Oven where pottery is fired at a low temperature, after the application of colored decoration, to fix the decoration and make it durable.

Decorator: A person who applies color to a piece of ware that already has had a design placed on it.

Designer: A person who makes a drawing, plan, or sketch to serve as a pattern.

Encrustation: Decorative layer of costly material.

English Ball Clay: Type of clay found in England; incorporated into ceramic bodies to give them plasticity during shaping.

Engraving: A method of decoration. In its application to the ceramic field, engraving may refer to the process of incising the desired design on a copper cylinder. When the design has been colored or inked, it can then be transferred to the ware by means of transfer paper. Engraved decoration is also that which is incised directly into the surface of the object being decorated.

Fat Oil: Turpentine that has been allowed to evaporate partially so that is thicker. When colors are mixed with it before being applied to an object, they will not run together.

Glaze: A glassy layer on the surface of a ceramic product achieved by applying a coating made up of certain specific materials and baking the article in a kiln until the coating has become hard and permanent.

Glost Kiln: Oven for baking glazed pieces for purpose of hardening the glaze.

Hand-Decorated: Colored by hand, though the pattern or design was applied by transfer print.

Hand-Painted: Decorated entirely by hand, both in design and coloring.

Jigger: Machine for shaping pottery by means of a tool fixed at a short distance from the surface of a plaster mold that is mechanically rotated on the head of a vertical spindle.

Jug: Container for liquids. Usually has a spout or narrow neck and a handle.

Junks: Pieces of clay cut out with a spade from the mass in the clay cellar after mellowing process.

Kaolin: Fine white firing clay consisting essentially of kaolinite.

Kiln: High-temperature oven used for firing of ceramic ware.

Lamelle: Buffalo Pottery trade name for type of ware with an inlaid center of clay, which, in combination with colored bodies, reinforces an article.

Lawn: Fine mesh screen or sieve through which the clay slip passes to remove impurities.

Liner: Person who places all the lines on the ware.

Lune Ware: Name given by Buffalo Pottery to blue solid-body vitreous china.

Medallion: An oval or circular design with relief carving, resembling a medal in shape.

Molds: Hollow form for shapping of pottery.

Multifleure: Buffalo Pottery trade name for a type of ware that utilized five different colored clays, resulting in marblelike effect.

Overglaze Decoration: Decoration applied to pottery after it has been glazed. The ware is again fired and the colors fuse onto the glaze, the decoration becoming durable. Because the decorating fire can be at a lower temperature with overglaze decoration, a more varied palette of colors is available than with underglaze decoration.

Piecework: Incentive system whereby employees are paid by the amount of work they produce instead of an hourly or weekly salary.

Pitcher: A container for holding and pouring liquids, with a lip on one side and handle on the other.

Plaque: An ornamental tablet of pottery intended to be hung up as a wall decoration.

Porcelain: Fine, translucent hard earthenware with a transparent glaze; china.

Potter's Wheel: A rotating horizontal disk upon which clay is molded into dishes, etc.

Pottery: Any product made from fired clay.

Premium: A reward, especially one given as an incentive for purchasing items.

Print Shop: Department where decals and transfer prints are made and applied to ware.

Printing (Transfer Printing): Process of decoration by which a single colored pattern is transferred directly from a printing plate or roller by means of thin paper.

Pug Mill: A machine for consolidating plastic clay into a firm column.

Pulldown: Part of the jigger that holds the tool for shaping the ware.

Rococo: A period of art circa 1715–1760. Nature was the source of inspiration. Decoration was small and human in scale, as opposed to the monumental forms of the baroque. Flowers, especially roses, and rustic scenes are characteristic of rococo motifs.

Rouge Ware: Name given by Buffalo Pottery to pink solid-body vitreous ware.

Sagger: A fireclay box, usually oval, in which pottery ware can be set in the kiln, to protect the ware from contamination by kiln gases.

Second: Any piece of ware that has a slight imperfection. Ware classed as a third or fourth had more serious imperfections. Class was determined by an inspector.

Semiporcelain: An opaque porcelain with a finish like that of earthenware. Absorbs impurities and grease readily.

Semivitreous China: Same as semiporcelain china.

Slip: A suspension in water of clay or other ceramic materials, used for casting in molds.

Solid Body Colors: Colors that are consistent throughout the entire piece of ware.

Steel Engraving: Etched design on a steel plate or roller.

Stove Room: Room that is heated slightly to remove moisture from the clay after it has been molded.

Suspension: A mixture in which very small particles of a solid remain suspended without dissolving.

Tankard: Tall mug, usually with a handle and hinged cover.

Tennessee Ball Clay: A clay found in Tennessee that is incorporated in ceramic bodies to give them plasticity during shaping and vitrification during firing.

Transfer Print: Tissue paper on which a sticky ink design has been applied and will be transferred to the bisque ware.

Turner: Person who forms things or shapes a substance on a lathe.

Underglaze Decoration: Decoration applied to pottery before it has been glazed. Because it is finally covered by the glaze, such decorations are completely durable. The subsequent glost firing is at such a high temperature that the range of available colors for decoration is limited.

Vitrified China: A strong high-grade ceramic ware fired at a high temperature to a glasslike finish. Has a low water-absorption rate.

Whirler: Hand-operated turntable upon which plaster molds are placed. Pieces not perfectly round are formed on whirlers.

Ye Olde Ivory: Name given by Buffalo Pottery to ivory solid-body vitreous china.

Bibliography

Booklets

Andrews, Peter C., "The Canadian Shore," *Adventures in Western New York History,* Volume XIV, Western New York Foundation, 1966.

Bown, W. E., "Buffalo Pottery Salesman Book," Buffalo Pottery, Buffa'o.

"Buffalo Pottery Blue Willow," Buffalo Pottery, Buffalo.

"Chesapeake and Ohio Railway Annual Report," Cleveland, 1959.

"China—Its Origin and Manufacture," Buffalo Pottery, Buffalo.

Harland, Marion, *My Trip Through the Larkin Factories,* Larkin Company, Buffalo, 1913.

Martin, Darwin, "The Larkin Office Was the First to Make a Card Ledger," Buffalo, 1932.

"The Famous Barberini-Portland Vase," Buffalo Pottery, Buffalo, 1946.

"The Potter's Art," Larkin Company, Buffalo, 1905.

Books

Dodd, A. E., *Dictionary of Ceramics,* Philosophical Library, New York, 1964.

Hill, Henry W., *Municipality of Buffalo—A History,* Volume I, Lewis Historical Publishing Company, Inc., New York, 1923.

Magazines

Gernert, Dee Albert, "Buffalo Pottery's Deldare Ware," *Spinning Wheel,* March, 1963.

The Live Wire (Journal of Commerce, Niagara Area), Volume 2, Number I, 1910.

Newspapers

Buffalo Courier Express, October 24, 1902; December 4, 1902; January 11, 1903; May 29, 1904; March 19, 1927; July 6, 1930; January 28, 1938; November 11, 1940.

Buffalo Evening News, July 8, 1902; April 12, 1939; October 4, 1939; March 28, 1940; April 25, 1940; May 16, 1940; November 23, 1940; January 15, 1947; April 3, 1965.

Illustrated Express, October 11, 1908.

Buffalo China's China Clipper, Volume I, Number I, November, 1964.

Industry in Buffalo and Niagara Frontier Scrap Book, Volumes 3, 4, 5.

Thesis

Schlei, Mildred B., "The Larkin Company," 1932.

Index